For Mark Dubovsky

with affection

Mark Osram

The Need to Believe

THE NEED TO BELIEVE

The Psychology of Religion

By

MORTIMER OSTOW, M.D., Med.Sc.D.

and

BEN-AMI SCHARFSTEIN, Ph.D.

INTERNATIONAL UNIVERSITIES PRESS, INC.

NEW YORK   NEW YORK

The authors wish to thank Professors Horace Friess and Herbert Schneider, and Dr. Marguerite Block, all of Columbia University, for their friendliness in reading and commenting on our book. Our views should not, of course, be attributed to them.

The Princeton University Press has given us permission to quote J. C. Archer's The Sikhs; *Random House, to quote Lin Yutang's* Wisdom of India and China; *Schocken Books, to quote G. Scholem's* Major Trends in Jewish Mysticism; *and the Macmillan Company, to quote J. B. Pratt's* Pilgrimage of Buddhism.

We wish to thank these authors and publishers, as well as such as are not mentioned here explicitly, but to whom we owe equal gratitude.

Contents

Introduction

PSYCHIATRY and religion are at odds, or seem to be. Current literature leaves the impression that they are glaring at one another watchfully, like enemies in the quiet moment before they come to grips. To avert the danger, some writers try to persuade the two that they are friends at heart, while others grant psychiatry its place, but only a subordinate one, for they hold that it has fallen into pride and arrogated to itself a power that it cannot rightfully exercise.

As we say during the course of the book, we believe that psychiatry, or, more narrowly, psychoanalysis, has a particular job of healing to do, whereas religion invigorates and directs in a general way. Psychoanalysis is aimed at individual neurotic problems and religion at the unhappiness inherent in human life as we know it. But the psychoanalytic principles established in the treatment of patients can illuminate the whole of our lives, including religion. Rather than serve partisan needs, we prefer to explain what the analyst has discovered about religion as a social phenomenon and a personal expression. At the end we state what we think of the relevance of his discoveries to the partisan argument.

It is impossible to be altogether objective, but we are interested in describing the workings of religion, not in lauding or condemning it. In order to encourage a spirit of calm appraisal, the reasoning is often illustrated with examples from other cultures, which are far enough away to weaken the feeling of personal involvement.

Analytical theory deals with all the chief aspects of human experience. In many areas the theory is incomplete and in others doubtful. Even where it is proved, in the sense that any clinical inferences can be empirically validated, the theory becomes abstruse, and to many people without earlier knowledge of it, decidedly implausible. But we have made no attempt to defend analysis, believing that no defense is called for, and that the book's reason for being is to present the conclusions of analysis as it stands. As Freud says in his *Outline of Psychoanalysis*, an independent judgment of the theory can be made only by those who have a first-hand acquaintance with the data on which it is based.

We have drawn freely on the entire body of psychoanalytic literature, especially on Freud. There are more detailed presentations of some of the subject matter in Freud's *Mourning and Melancholia, Totem and Taboo, Moses and Monotheism, The Future of an Illusion,* and *Civilization and Its Discontents*; in Flugel's *Men, Morals and Society*; in Reik's *Psychoanalytic Studies of Ritual*; and in Nunberg's *Problems of Bisexuality as Reflected in Circumcision*.

To bring the ideas within the realm of ordinary experience, we have taken advantage of only those parts of psychoanalytic theory which pertain directly to the subject. Nowhere have we aimed at the rigor needed to establish conviction, but it has been our aim to write clearly and understandably. In a summary of this kind we have had to approximate, schematize, drive points home by example rather than full exposition, and commit other sins that are, in their place, natural, venial, and maybe even good.

CHAPTER 1

The Link Between Psychiatry and Religion

IT MAY seem strange that psychiatry should be supposed to have any relevance whatever to religion. Psychiatry is a branch of clinical medicine dealing with the description, recognition, and treatment of disease. Yet psychiatry has always been considered to be different from other medical fields. Until very recently it was included in the curricula of only a few medical schools. Although most practicing physicians look on themselves as unskilled in psychiatric diagnosis, many of them believe they can give adequate psychotherapy. In fact, many laymen think themselves qualified to pass judgment on the current psychiatric theories. To some extent psychiatrists encourage this delusion by publishing important contributions in books addressed to the laity as well as to their colleagues. Books of essentially psychiatric interest are more often assigned for review to nonprofessionals than to men in the field.

The truth is that psychiatry has become an authentic branch of medicine only during the past century and a half. It has been difficult for laymen and even physicians to realize that unusual behavior can be considered a clinical abnormality. The recognition of unusual behavior itself was little less astute in ancient days than it is at present. But the explanations then given were neither revealing nor helpful, nor are the best current ones really satisfactory.

It is interesting that psychiatrists should now be engaged in throwing light upon religion, when, in the past, religion was thought to have the function of understanding and managing disorders of the spirit. The theories of demonology and witchcraft, so highly developed during the Middle Ages, were concerned with psychic illness. The *Malleus Maleficarum*, the *Witch Hammer*, the most authoritative medieval book on witchcraft, first published about 1486, declared that impotence, "injury to the use of reason," and "tormenting of the inner perceptions," including obsessive love and hatred, were caused by witchcraft. It recommended that cures be effected through pilgrimages to holy places, confession, prayer, the sign of the cross, lawful exorcism, and the like. Medicines and music may seem to cure psychic troubles, said the *Malleus*, but without religion they are not enough:

> The devil, moving only in local vapour of the spirit, can grievously afflict men supernaturally. But herbs and harmonies cannot of their own natural virtue cause in man a disposition by which the devil is prevented from creating the commotion. . . . And as for that concerning *I Kings* xvi: that Saul, who was vexed by a devil, was alleviated when David played his harp before him, and that the devil departed, etc. It must be known that it is quite true that by the playing of the harp, and the natural virtue of that harmony, the affliction of Saul was to some extent relieved, inasmuch as that music did somewhat calm his sense through hearing; through which calming he was made less prone to that vexation.

> But the reason why the evil spirit departed when David played the harp was because of the might of the Cross, which is clearly enough shown by the gloss, where it says: David was learned in music, skilful in the different notes and harmonic modulations. He shows the essential unity by playing each day in various modes. David repressed the evil spirit by the harp, not because there was so much virtue in the harp, but it was made in the sign of a cross, being a cross of wood with the strings stretched across. And even at that time the devils fled from this.[1]

During the Middle Ages it became the duty of the religious inquisition to deal with mental abnormalities. To this very day many men of religion are reluctant to surrender to the psychiatrist's care anyone who is not grossly insane. Many psychiatrists as well as religious leaders persist in comparing the methods of psychiatric therapy with the methods of religion, as though religion were a psychotherapeutic procedure, or psychotherapy had the role of dealing with the everyday ethical and emotional problems of normal people.

What is the rightful province of the psychiatrists? Although observations on mental illness appeared in the earliest medical writings, including those of Hippocrates and Galen, it was not until the end of the eighteenth century that the physician began to insist that the treatment of the lunatic was a medical problem, and that the lunatic asylum should be organized as a mental hospital. The lunatics were people whose behavior was so bizarre that they were wholly incapable of dealing with the problems of daily living. They included patients whom we now call psychotic, as well as the seriously feeble-minded.

[1] *Malleus Maleficarum,* translated by M. Summers, London, 1928, p. 41.

The essential characteristic of psychotics is the loss of contact with reality, that is, of the ability to distinguish between the real world and the world of fantasy, so that behavior becomes inappropriate and even dangerous to themselves or others. The essential characteristic of the feeble-minded is the lack of enough intelligence to deal with even the minor and regular problems of life.

In some cases of such seriously abnormal behavior, organic disease of the brain was observed at the autopsy table. In these cases the relationship between psychiatry and the rest of medicine became particularly intimate. Usually, however, no clear-cut abnormality of the brain could be demonstrated, and has not been demonstrated to this day.

Descriptions of people with epileptic spells have come down to us from ancient times. The fact that convulsive movements reflect a disturbance of the physiology of the brain has brought the disease within the purview of modern medicine. Some of the most seriously affected epileptics behave queerly or are grossly feeble-minded. For this reason the psychiatrist too became interested in the disease, and epileptics are still looked on as proper subjects for admission into mental hospitals.

As the nineteenth century wore on and physicians turned more and more to the study of abnormalities of behavior, they were approached for treatment by many individuals who showed no serious loss of contact with the real world, but whose lives were made miserable by symptoms that could not be understood. Such individuals were called psychoneurotics.

Most people are familiar with the broad general types of psychoneurosis. The hysteric, for example, suffers from dramatic symptoms of the kind usually caused by serious

14

physical disease, symptoms such as paralysis, blindness, deafness, or numbness of a certain part of the body. But no physical disease can be found in cases of hysteria, and the symptoms will often yield to simple measures like hypnosis or other forms of suggestion.

The person with an anxiety neurosis finds himself frequently and unaccountably fearful, apprehensive, tremulous, sleepless, and unable to think clearly. Some individuals develop attacks of anxiety only under fairly specific circumstances, in subways, for example, or in other confining enclosures.

There are also people whose minds are filled during most of their waking hours with uncomfortable thoughts such as those of hurting family or friends. Other people wash their hands a hundred times a day, feel they must get dressed in a certain elaborate order, or perform other acts with great intensity and ritualistic exactness. Often the uncomfortable thoughts and ritualistic acts occur together, for which reason either of them alone is usually assumed to be the mark of an obsessive-compulsive neurosis. Then there is the hypochondriac, who is plagued by the false conviction that he is physically ill, and the neurasthenic, who, though he has rested, always feels too weak and tired to fulfill the day's obligations.

Once these psychoneuroses, which had not previously been thought of as diseases, were carefully described, it became evident that they affected much more of the population than did the psychoses. The psychiatrists now found themselves dealing with large numbers of unhappy men and women who had not hitherto been considered ill. It was only during the twentieth century that psychiatrists began to recognize that there were many people without the symptoms even of psychoneurosis who went through life intensely unhappy. Again and again they acted in a manner, as a disinterested observer could see, that was virtually calculated to end in misfortune. Such people are said to have character or personality disorders. For instance, there are those who no matter how healthy, attractive, intelligent, and even rich, fail in every undertaking. There are the charming women who seem never to be able to find the right husband. The psychiatrist feels obligated to treat this kind of internally caused unhappiness as a medical disorder.

Through this simple historic evolution the psychiatrist was forced to turn from his exclusive preoccupation with the problems of the "lunatic" to much of the world's unhappiness, and to the treatment of men heretofore considered to be inept, unfortunate, and pitiable, but scarcely ill.

The range of psychiatry as we have described it is hardly very limited. Nevertheless, some psychiatrists have staked a claim in every sphere of human activity. They have said that psychiatrists should be appointed to governmental bodies to assist in reaching decisions on the economic and social welfare of entire nations. Some psychiatrists feel that they should take the place of priests, some that they know how to stop wars. *Nil humanum mihi alienum est.*

Not all unhappiness can be ascribed to emotional maladjustment. The person who does not grieve at the death of a loved one is more likely to be mentally ill than the person who does. When the melancholy lasts too long, however, the depression must be considered pathological, and the help of the psychiatrist rather than the clergyman invoked. The inability to find work in times of economic depression is not a mark of character disorder, although a man who finds it hard to get a job will often

16

blame economic difficulties when his emotional difficulties are the real source of his trouble. When social upheavals are provoked in part by the emotional disorders of powerful leaders, the psychiatrist may be able to put his finger on a focus of the disturbance. But wars are often initiated and conducted by the sound, calculating minds of leaders who hope to gain their own or their nation's selfish ends.

There are, therefore, many kinds of unhappiness the psychiatrist cannot directly treat as he treats someone who is ill. On the other hand, as a result of his work with the abnormal, the psychiatrist gains insight into the psychology of the normal person. This insight can be put to good use in every field of human endeavor, not through the assumption of a doctor's authority over his patient, but through the illumination of the modes and motives of human behavior. It is in such a sense that we think that psychiatry can illuminate religion.

The statement that an understanding of abnormal behavior leads to an understanding of the normal psyche may sound like an unwarranted generalization. How can it be justified?

Irrationality is a constant aspect of neurotic and psychotic behavior. The paranoid may believe that his family and closest friends are plotting to murder him, when no real basis for the suspicion can be found. The depressed patient may consider himself responsible for harming his family, when there is no reason to believe so. The paralyses, anxieties, and depressions of neurotics cannot be understood in terms of any explanation the patient is able to give. The problem that presented itself to the nineteenth-century psychiatrist was this: if he were to do more than describe mental illness, he had to work out some theory that would at least explain the available data, if

17

not provide a framework on which to base an intelligent therapy.

The task was attempted by many of the theoreticians of fifty and seventy-five years ago. Only Freud succeeded in going beyond mere description. He recognized that irrational behavior was not limited to the mentally ill, but that, on the contrary, many aspects of the behavior of normal individuals were as opaque to intelligence as the delusions of the insane. Why do people persist in clinging to superstitions that others around them know are unjustified? How can we account for personal, religious, and racial bias even in communities that profess a democratic ideal? What determines the irrational nature of daydreams? Why is it that some people who are alert and healthy have one accident after another? Why are there constant tensions and emotional crises in families living under no economic or social strain? What is the meaning of dreams?

Freud believed that we could never begin to answer these questions, nor to understand psychic abnormality, so long as we accepted at face value the motives with which one usually explains one's behavior. He preferred to assume that what goes on in the mind of anyone is not limited to what he talks about or to what he consciously thinks. The theory of unconscious mental activity gave the first revealing insight into unreasoned behavior.

How did Freud achieve the insight? There were several methods that proved especially useful. One method is no more than the evaluation of a patient's motives in terms of his actions rather than his claims. The pretty girl who says she cannot find a suitable husband must be suspected of trying to avoid marriage, though not consciously aware that she is. The censor who eagerly reads prurient books for the good, as he thinks, of the public, must be suspected of unconsciously seeking the very gratification he wants to deny to others.

A second method is the use of free association. When a person is asked to recite without any form of selection all that comes to his mind, the observer will often find a nuclear concern in the recital of which the person is not consciously aware. It is common for a psychoanalyst, just before he leaves on a vacation, to hear his patients recall unsuccessful love affairs, instances of rejection by their parents or unfair treatment by teachers, broken engagements and divorces of friends, and so on and so forth. A patient of this sort is taking the analyst's departure as a personal rejection. If the patient is asked whether he is preoccupied with any particular feeling, he will deny that there is a relationship among the memories that have risen in his mind. Yet if he is told, "You resent my leaving, just as you resented your father's leaving you as a child, an experience you now remember, and you feel rejected," he is likely to answer, "Well, yes, I was quite annoyed when you told me of your plans to leave the city."

In the course of an analysis of an unmarried girl, it sometimes happens that she will spend a session talking about surgical operations, blood, and friends who are pregnant. If asked whether her period is late this month, she will answer in surprise, "Yes, how did you know?" Obviously, the girl is concerned, to an extent she may not consciously realize, with the possibility of an unwelcome pregnancy.

A third approach that Freud used was an examination of the circumstances under which meaningful errors occur. For example, when a girl you know to be jealous of her brother's privileges as a boy introduces herself with the words "I am Al's brother" instead of "I am Al's sister," it

19

is reasonable to infer that she really wishes she were somebody's brother. One of the authors remembers that a girl he had been seeing once called him by the name of another fellow, who had been courting her simultaneously. He was not surprised to receive an announcement two weeks later of her engagement to his rival. And who does not know that a fellow who forgets to appear for a date can have little desire to meet his girl?

One of the most revealing methods to discover unconscious motives is the interpretation of dreams. As the result of much clinical experience, Freud contended that every dream represents in a distorted form the fulfillment of a wish that is inacceptable to the conscious waking mind. Although the material of a dream is usually taken from the easily recalled events of the past few days, the wish responsible for the formation of the dream is not consciously acknowledged by the dreamer.

A patient dreamed that he was lining up with his old army company, and the image of the sergeant barking out orders was especially vivid. On the evening before the dream he had had a falling out with his wife that led him to regret having married. He recalled that he had enlisted in the army after some difficulty with a previous girl friend. His dream was interpreted to him in this way: "You escaped the dangerous designs of a woman by joining an exclusively male group, the army. Now you have become disgusted with marriage and you hope once again to be relieved of the oppression by joining the company of men, especially of the analyst. His analytic instructions are represented by the instructions of the sergeant. Even though it involves subordinating yourself, you would rather be emotionally related to a man than a woman."

These are the techniques Freud used to gain an understanding of psychic illness. Through them he was able to devise a helpful method of treatment, and finally, with their assistance, he tried to understand the otherwise incomprehensible behavior of normal people, both as individuals and as groups.

With the treatment of mental illness we are not concerned here. It is a matter, after all, for discussion among psychiatrists, since only they are able to evaluate the suggested methods. We want to use the interpretive technique of psychoanalysis to clarify religion.

CHAPTER 2

Theories on the Nature of Religion

THAT this book concentrates on one approach to religion does not imply that we regard others as less legitimate. Like all the expressions of human life that have developed over the course of many thousands of years, religious belief has a multitude of aspects. There are as many answers to the question, "What is religion?" as there are philosophies and social sciences.

Time-honored answers are those that have been given by the philosophers. Some philosophers have attacked religion; the vast majority, who have lived in a highly religious environment, have defended one or another of its forms; and some have been neutral. The philosophical answers are generally marked by their bold speculation. They are so comprehensive and attempt to penetrate so deeply that they often go beyond even the possibility of inductive proof. It is out of our province to review the relations of philosophy with religion, but the answer of a famous recent philosopher, Henri Bergson, may be a suggestive example. It somewhat approximates Carl Jung's, which is discussed in the concluding chapter.

According to Bergson, if there were not a preventive rudiment of instinct, a primitively intelligent man would rush to help himself to all the pleasures that enticed him.

The instinct protects him from his own selfishness by the invention of an unrational mythology that keeps him social. Religion, that is, is nature's defense against the selfish, destructive, antisocial power of primitive intelligence. Religion is also a natural defense against man's knowledge that he must die. The fear of death is counteracted by the ideas of souls, ghosts, and spirits. Intelligence has a native pessimism. It knows that we cannot foresee the results of our actions. Religion gives the future an optimistic coloring.

But all this defensive religion is radically limited. It is static, confined, and uncreative. Side by side with it there has always been a surging creativity, a love, and a positive desire to share. Around our intelligence is an ancient fringe of intuition, through which the true mystic or prophet is able to know what lies beyond the world of separate material things. Our intelligence is alert to defend us against a variety of dangers. It has been evolved as a practical instrument, and it misses the immaterial and essential impulse of life. For there is a god, a wholly creative force: we are its creations and our creations express its creativity. If we learn to go beyond our intelligence into the joy that is active, intuitive, and mystically intense, we will rise from beneath the burden of our material progress. We will feel how each separate one of us shares in an indissoluble union. Together we will surge forward on this refractory planet, whose stubborn resistance can serve a humanity united in mystical energy to become godlike.

We have already disclaimed our intention to make or judge such bold claims. They are crucially important, beyond a doubt, and on them rests the final truth of religion as commonly understood. By their very nature, however, they have escaped, and will perhaps continue to escape, factual proof or disproof. The evidence is not alone insufficient to establish the truth of the philosophic theories, it is also not enough to validate the more modest judgments of the social sciences.

Consider, for example, the religion of the ancient Greeks. It has been studied intensively for centuries; and yet the man who is regarded as the greatest modern authority on Greek religion, Martin P. Nilsson, has said that the comprehensive works on Greek mythology are almost entirely defective. Or consider the critical evidence that comes from the study of primitive life. The early observers of primitives were naturally not as systematic or careful as the best of the modern anthropologists. But the faults of the early observers can never be rectified because some of the primitives have died out and the lives of most of the others have been transformed.

One of the mistakes made by early observers and still sometimes repeated is the assumption that the account given by a priest or medicine man holds good for the entire group. Usually there are a learned, priestly religion, an indefinite popular religion, and personal idiosyncrasies of all kinds. We who have authoritative scriptures and unified churches find it hard to realize that in many parts of the world there has not been a clearly established authoritative form of the prevailing religion. There was no Greek religion in the sense that there is a Catholic one.

When the data are missing, or vague and variable, factually justified conclusions are hard to reach. However, there have been, of course, many hypotheses that have commanded a following among anthropologists.

In the presence of natural phenomena which could not be explained or controlled physically, plausible explanations were developed. By couching these explanations in

the familiar terms of human relations, the unknown became a part of the supposedly known. In addition, one
now had a magical technique for influencing the processes
of nature.

One popular, long-lived theory was that the gods and
spirits of religion were personifications of the sun, moon,
rain, lightning, and other heavenly bodies and forces. The
primitive tendency to personify is characteristic of children. A little deaf and dumb boy, isolated because of his
affliction from the ideas of other people, later reported on
his speculations:

> Nothing stimulated his curiosity like the
> moon. He was afraid of the moon, but he loved
> to watch her. He noticed the shadowy face in the
> full moon. Then he supposed she was a living
> being. So he tried to prove whether the moon was
> alive or not. It was accordingly done in four dif-
> ferent ways. First he shook his head in a zig-zag
> direction, with his eyes fixed on the moon. She
> appeared to follow the motions of his head, now
> rising and then lowering, turning forward and
> backward. He also thought that the lights were
> alive too, because he repeated similar experi-
> ments. Secondly, while walking out, he watched
> whether the moon would follow him. The orb
> seemed to follow him everywhere. Thirdly, he
> wondered why the moon appeared regularly. So
> he thought she must have come out to see him
> alone. Then he talked to her in gestures and
> fancied that he saw her smile or frown. Fourthly,
> he found that he had been whipped oftener
> when the moon was visible. It was as though she
> were watching him and telling his guardian (he
> being an orphan boy) all about his bad capers.
> He often asked himself who she could be. At
> last he became sure she was his mother, because,

while his mother lived, he had never seen the moon. Afterwards, every now and then, he saw the moon and behaved well towards his friends.[2]

The nature deities of religion have had a more complicated origin than this, but at bottom there must have been a similar process of reasoning. The Indians, Persians, Greeks, Romans, Scandinavians, and others, have had great sun-gods. The Persians and Indians (of India) worshiped the god of fire. The thunderstorm was personified as Zeus, Jupiter, and Thor. All these became deities because they attracted the wondering eye of their viewers, and because they were of obviously overwhelming importance to communities prevailingly agricultural. If the Nile overflowed too little or too much, it was a disaster, and the Egyptians, who could of course do nothing to change the degree of the overflow, felt that the Nile was a living being whose friendship must be kept. And the sun was to them a golden force of life that sustained all life with its beneficent, fruitful heat.

Another, more general, and still more popular theory was that of animism, which was made famous by the Englishman, E. B. Tylor, in a work first issued in 1872. He thought that primitives developed the idea of a human soul from dreams and visions, in which a life-principle seemed to be undergoing experiences not shared by the body. In ecstasy, sleep, sickness, and death, the body and the principle of life seemed to be separated too. Thus arose the belief in life after death and in transmigration. Primitive man was unable to conceive of other things except on the model of himself, and so just as he ascribed

---

[2] The speculations of the deaf and dumb boy were reported by William James in 1892 in an article called "Thought before Language." The present paragraph is requoted from Pierre Bovet, *The Child's Religion*, New York, 1928, pp. 66-67.

a soul to his own body, he ascribed souls to animals and plants, and then to other, inanimate things as well. Then there followed the conception of pure spirits, which were the souls of dead ancestors, and which might enter the bodies of other persons and cause sickness or death.

According to Tylor, nature was believed to be inhabited by souls, and men began to worship the spirits of the waters, the trees, and the beasts. When single animals, such as the serpent, were worshiped it became possible to imagine an inclusive species' serpent-god. In this way, the more advanced groups arrived at the idea of gods with some general power—a rain-god, a thunder-god, a sun-god, a moon-god, a god of agriculture, a god of war, and so on. Finally, either one of the nature gods or the primal ancestral god became the head of the rest of them. The others were ranged below him in order of importance like the officials of a government. It also happened that the powers of nature were fused into one vague, all-pervading, and altogether exalted and remote supreme deity.

Whatever the modifications that Tylor's theory must undergo, there are many convincing examples of animism. A four-year-old child who knocks into a chair becomes angry at it and kicks it. The child has come to recognize animosity. He believes that that which causes him pain is an enemy, and an enemy is a person. When he was six, Edmund Gosse, later to become a well-known English writer, used to imagine spells to make the birds and butterflies in his father's illustrated manuals come alive and fly away, leaving holes in the book behind them. A child connects movement with life. The clouds may seem to him to be alive and flying, the trees to be waving their arms, and the leaves to be dancing. Children also naturally elaborate notions of ghostlike beings. The English essayist,

Walter Pater, tells how he got these notions from some chance remarks he heard soon after the terrible event of his father's death:

> For sitting one day in the garden below an open window, he heard people talking, and could not but listen, how, in a sleepless hour, a sick woman had seen one of the dead sitting beside her, come to call her hence; and from the broken talk evolved with much clearness the notion that not all those dead people had really departed to the churchyard, nor were quite so motionless as they looked, but led a secret, half-fugitive life in their old homes, quite free by night, though sometimes visible in the day, dodging from room to room, with no great goodwill towards those who shared the place with them. All night the figure sat beside him in the reveries of his broken sleep, and was not quite gone in the morning —an odd, irreconcilable new member of the household, making the sweet familiar chambers unfriendly and suspect by its uncertain presence. He could have hated the dead he had pitied so, for being thus. Afterwards he came to think of those poor, home-returning ghosts, which all men have fancied to themselves—the *revenants*— pathetically, as crying, or beating with vain hands at the doors, as the wind came, their cries distinguishable in it as a wilder inner note.[3]

Primitives and children are certainly not the same— primitives have a cultural history—but it is striking to see the qualities of Pater's ghosts duplicated in primitive ghosts, grotesque, occasionally visible existences that are dangerous, and that inspire uneasiness though they may be called upon for help.

Among the competitors of the theory of animism was

[3] Walter Pater, "The Child in the House," in *Miscellaneous Studies*.

that of totemism. The latter theory drew on the former, but was more narrowly explicit. One of the early influential exponents of totemism was W. Robertson Smith, whose books appeared in the late nineteenth century. Smith was interested mainly in the Semitic religions, above all in the Hebrew. He said that primitives believed that a certain animal, a god, and a tribe, might be of the same ancestry. Usually it was forbidden to sacrifice the tribal animal. But on certain solemn festivals, the totemic animal, which also represented the god, was killed and eaten. Its flesh and blood were believed to renew the communion and vitality of those who shared in the feast. This theory of totemism served Sigmund Freud as the basis of his own explanation of the origin of religion. It also served the famous French sociologist, Emile Durkheim.

Totemism is characteristic of the Eskimo, for example. Franz Boas, who knew them well, reported:

> The Eskimo who inhabit the coasts of arctic America subsist mainly by the chase of sea mammals, such as seals of various kinds, walruses, and whales. Whenever this source of supply is curtailed, want and famine sets in. The huts are cold and dark—for heat and light are obtained by burning the blubber of seals and whales—and soon the people succumb to the terrors of the rigorous climate. For this reason the native does everything in his power to gain the good will of the sea mammals and to insure success in hunting. All his thoughts are bent upon treating them in such a manner that they may allow themselves to be caught. On this account they form one of the main subjects of his religious beliefs and customs. They play a most important part in his mythology, and a well-nigh endless series of observances regulates their treatment.

The observances are allied with the belief of the Eskimo that a woman, Sedna, fled in her father's boat to escape her husband. The husband pursued, and her father threw her overboard. She clung to the gunwale, but her father chopped off her finger joints, which became seals, ground seals, and whales.

> This woman, the mother of the sea mammals, may be considered the principal deity of the Central Eskimo. She has supreme sway over the destinies of mankind, and almost all the observances of these tribes are for the purpose of retaining her good will or of propitiating her if she has been offended. Among the eastern tribes of this region she is called Sedna, while the tribes of Hudson Bay call her Nuliayuk. She is believed to live in a lower world, in a house built of stone and whale ribs. The souls of seals, ground seals, and whales are believed to proceed from her house. After one of these animals has been killed its soul stays with the body for three days. Then it goes back to Sedna's abode, to be sent forth again by her. If, during the three days that the soul stays with the body, any tabu or prescribed custom is violated, the violation becomes attached to the animal's soul. Although the latter strives to free itself of these attachments, which give it pain, it is unable to do so, and takes them down to Sedna. The attachments, in some manner that is not explained, make her hands sore, and she punishes the people who are the cause of her pains by sending to them sickness, bad weather and starvation. The object of the innumerable tabus that are in force after the killing of the sea animals is therefore to keep their souls free from attachments that would hurt their souls as well as Sedna.[4]

[4] F. Boas, "Religious Beliefs of the Central Eskimo," *Popular Science Monthly*, 57, pp. 624-27. In W. I. Thomas, *Primitive Behavior*, New York, 1937, p. 600.

In addition to the theories of animism and totemism, there is also the concept of *mana*. *Mana* is a Polynesian and Melanesian term that has been used to characterize the primitive belief, supposed by the extreme adherents of the theory to be universal, in a mysterious magical force that permeates the world and is the cause of at least all exceptional happenings. In the words of the best known description of the concept:

> The Melanesian mind is entirely possessed by the belief in a supernatural power or influence, called almost universally *mana*. . . . It is present in the atmosphere of life, attaches itself to persons and to things, and is manifested by results which can only be ascribed to its operation. When one has got it he can use and direct it, but its force may break forth at some new point; the presence of it is ascertained by proof. A man comes by chance upon a stone which takes his fancy; its shape is singular, it is like something, it is certainly not a common stone, there must be mana in it. So he argues with himself, and he puts it to the proof; he lays it at the root of a tree to the fruit of which it has a certain resemblance, or he buries it in the ground when he plants his garden; an abundant crop on the tree or in the garden shows that he is right, the stone is mana, has that power in it. Having that power it is a vehicle to convey mana to other stones. . . . All conspicuous success is a proof that a man has mana; his influence depends on the impression made on the people's mind that he has it; he becomes a chief by virtue of it. Hence a man's power, though political or social in its character, is his mana; the word is naturally used in accordance with the native conception of the character of all power and influence as supernatural. If a man has been successful in fighting, it has not been his natural strength of arm, quickness of eye

or readiness of resource that has won success; he has certainly got the mana of a spirit or of some deceased warrior to empower him, conveyed in an amulet of a stone round his neck, or a tuft of leaves in his belt, in a tooth hung upon a finger of his bow hand, or in the form of words with which he brings supernatural assistance to his side. If a man's pigs multiply, and his gardens are productive, it is not because he is industrious and looks after his property, but because of the stones full of mana for pigs and yams that he possesses.[5]

Each of the foregoing theories was evolutionary. That is to say, it was thought that primitives began with childish, unformulated beliefs that developed into some kind of polytheism and gradually rose to monotheism. In the last decades, however, Wilhelm Schmidt, an immoderately learned but only moderately circumspect scholar, has been developing almost the opposite view. He thinks that the evidence points to a primeval monotheism. The most primitive men need to believe in a supreme god. They need him as an explanation of the cause of the universe, as the father of mankind to whom they owe allegiance, and as the morally perfect lawgiver and protector, to whom they can consign their fate. The most primitive men have been on the whole decent and morally strong. But as other gods and as demons were invented, as external civilization grew more splendid and temples, priests, and ceremonies were multiplied, the vitality of religion was often sapped and its original purity degraded. Schmidt, in other words, partly reinstates the old conception of an original golden age of mankind.

Contemporary anthropologists make more or less cautious syntheses of these and other theoretical formulations.

[5] R. H. Codrington, *The Melanesians*, 1891, pp. 118-120.

No single theory has come near commanding universal assent.

There is a point of view not very remote from that of anthropology, sometimes, indeed, indistinguishable from it, the point of view of sociology. Sociology is concerned with the behavior of groups of men. It deals with questions, among others, of this type: How does it come about that religions are organized into churches, sects, denominations, and secret societies? What is the nature of such groups? Who bears religious authority, and what is its origin and character? What is the nature and function of the founder of a religion, or a religious reformer, a seer, a medicine man, a prophet, a saint, a priest? What is the social function of myth, doctrine, and worship? How is religion related to social standing and to economics? Is one religion predominantly a peasant religion, a second a warrior religion, and a third an urban religion?

Since the advent of Marxism, the connection between religion and economics has been the subject of especial interest. It is true, to approach the question on its simplest level, that primitive medicine men may be aware that to maintain their place they have to inculcate the practices that heighten their prestige as magicians and intermediaries with the spirit world. It is also true that great churches have economic influence and that doctrine is often tinged, consciously or not, by the material interests of the authorities. But rather than to go on in such generalities, it may be better to summarize one investigation into the partnership between religion and economy.

Max Weber, the German sociologist, tried to show an interaction between early Protestant doctrine and the growth of capitalism. R. H. Tawney, the economic historian, illustrated and modified Weber's thesis. In the

33

Middle Ages, as Tawney said, no sharp line was drawn between the fields of religion and economics. Economic goods were distinctly secondary to the attainment of a virtuous life. Economic motives were regarded as ministering to base appetites, and were therefore suspected and surrounded with restrictions. The merchant was held in suspicion. Unlike the craftsman, who worked to live and earned no more than he needed, the merchant aimed at excess profit derived from mere buying and selling. He must be an immoral man, the Medievals thought, who buys cheaply in order to sell dearly, and who tries to disregard God's command that we should live by the sweat of our brows. And certainly he is immoral who is a money-lender and a leech. Even the banking houses that developed toward the end of the Middle Ages were inveighed against, though they were not as evidently oppressive as the moneylender who had immediate dealings with the little man.

Under the typical economic conditions of the Middle Ages it was possible to hold such a theory. Trading, money, and banking were not nearly as important as they later became. On the other hand, it was hard to denounce serfdom, on which the medieval economy depended. The Church on the whole accepted serfdom and went so far as to enforce it by canon law. But as capitalism developed, it grew plain that medieval morality was too restrictive and inapplicable to the new economic life. Calvin, for instance, distinguished between the interest wrung out of the poor and the interest a merchant might earn with borrowed money. In England, from the time of the Restoration, there were no further charges leveled against usury. Commerce, which was making England prosperous as never before, could not be the work of the devil. Religion narrowed its

34

claims and surrendered the field of business. It began, as in Puritanism, to emphasize diligence and thrift, and to regard the poor as at fault because self-indulgent and idle. This was a perfect rationalization for low wages and bad working conditions. It was said that the lower classes must be kept poor or they never would be industrious. In spite of notable exceptions, Puritanism completed the divorce between business and the traditional rules of ethics. Either religion was indifferent, or formulated its rules with an apt ambiguity that showed no precise application to commerce, finance, or the ownership of property. Religion had learned to answer the needs of an expanding commerce and industry.

Whether Tawney is right or not, it is a legitimate, revealing enterprise to examine the ways in which religion and economics affect one another. But there is another point of view, neither anthropological, historical, sociological, or economic, that is not less important than these. It may be called, broadly, the psychological. Even if religion has had the most crass economic motives, there are other, personal reasons why men accept a belief and find solace in worship. To find the reasons one must examine the inner life of the individual as his impulses find their modes of expression.

Freud tried to initiate the study of the psychological basis of religion by comparing it with the phenomena of primitive life. He was able to establish analogies between primitive, childhood, and neurotic behavior. With the acknowledgment that his theory could be no more than partial, Freud boldly reconstructed the prehistoric scene. He began with two facts. The Australian primitives, whom he regarded as about the most primitive in the world, were both totemistic and exogamous. That is, they revered totems and sternly prohibited anyone from marrying a person of the same totemic group. Could there be any essential connection between the customs of totemism and exogamy? Freud proceeded to explain that in the beginning, as Darwin held, people lived in groups governed by a violent, jealous father who kept all the women for himself and drove away the growing sons who might become his sexual rivals. But primitive men are not inhibited, and their desires are quickly converted into actions, and so, perhaps, the sons who had been expelled joined forces and killed their father. Like some modern cannibals and tribes that ceremonially eat the totem animal they identify with their ancestors, the sons ate their father. Like the primitives of today, they thought to share the ancestral strength in devouring the flesh in which it had resided. The totemic feast, which may have been the first celebration of men, is now a somewhat concealed repetition and commemoration of this crime. But the sons, with the feeling of a son who is moved by sexual love for his mother and rivalry against his father, were struck by remorse, because they had loved and admired as well as hated their father. Therefore they undid their deeds by prohibiting the killing of the animal that represented their father and renouncing the women they had acquired. This is the origin and the connection of the totemic and exogamous rules. Some people assume that there is a fundamental human instinct against incest. There cannot be any, for laws are passed to restrain men from doing as they wish. Therefore exogamy, which stems from a prohibition against incest, must be a restraint against the desire for incest. And the prohibition against killing the totemic animal must have answered the desire to kill the ancestor. That this is the origin of the two prohibitions is made

clear by the totemic feast, in which, for a sanctioned moment, the pent-up desire issues forth and sexual excesses
may be allowed. The belief in original sin preserves the
memory of the original crime. Since Christ redeems mankind by sacrificing his life, he must be expiating the only
crime that demands so great an expiation, murder. And
since the crime was committed against God, who is the
father, the crime must have been the murder of the father.
Thus Christianity is associated also with the renunciation
of women, the cause of the crime. But the son, in expiating
his deed, also attained the goal of his wishes. He became
God in place of the father-God. Then the other males,
through communion, shared the flesh and blood of the
son-God and became holy themselves.

All this is clearly hypothetical. Anthropologists have de-
nounced it as fantastic, and historians have refused to
accept Freud's similar reconstruction of the beginnings of
Judaism. But, still, we can agree that his approach has a
fundamentally sound element. Whatever forms history has
given to religion, religious and moral conceptions must
have a primal source in the deep, often unconscious drives
that lie behind our beliefs and practices. To work out the
historic consequences of these drives as they were deflected
by the environment in which they played themselves out
is an endless and delicate task that requires the combined
efforts of all the sciences. But with depth psychology we
begin at the beginning that remains always accessible to
us—the life of the single man. Without his loves and
hates, his wishes, wills, and aversions, there would be no
human society and no religion.

CHAPTER 3

The Energizing Forces of Religious Behavior

SOME of our wishes are active—we want to use another person to gratify ourselves—and we ordinarily acknowledge and even boast of them. We also have passive wishes —we want to be used, to have something done to us—and these we usually repudiate. In our society, the only passive wishes that are expected are the wishes of women for sexual gratification. But even these we understand silently rather than speak of openly. Yet we know from psychoanalysis that every primitive unconscious fantasy in which a person plays an active role alternates, in the same person, with another version of the fantasy in which the role becomes a passive one. This is equally true for men and women. These primitive fantasies, based on our nervous structure and early childhood experiences, remain unconscious. They express themselves, however, in conscious wishes and fantasies. All of us, men and women alike, harbor as many insistent passive as active wishes.

The passive wishes remain hidden, and any behavior to which they give rise is usually attributed to external compulsion. We suppose that we obey because we are forced to, and we ignore the possibility that we may want to obey. And yet we can recognize the wish to obey and to be mastered in every domestic animal. It is a good general principle that no living organism participates in any activity for which it does not have the psychic and neural equipment. If a creature obeys, it is because it has the equipment for obedience and even the tendency or wish to obey. Passivity implies more than obedience. A person wants to experience the passive counterpart of each of his active roles. When external compulsion cannot be given as an adequate cause, an ulterior motive is given instead. So, we permit ourselves to be acted on, we say, to gain favor, to disarm an opponent, to preserve peace, to be polite, to make money, to be treated for illness, and so on.

Why are passive wishes repudiated so energetically? There is a biological defense against passivity, because passive wishes indulged too far may give rise to a serious injury. For example, the animal that gives up too much to the leader of its pack may find itself without food, shelter, and a mate. The man who lets himself be acted upon becomes a prey to the aggressive impulses of others. At such a danger point, a warning signal appears, the signal of fear or, more generally, of anxiety. The person grows anxious and tries to abandon his passive role, either by fleeing or by shifting to an active role, by attacking his attacker, for instance. When there is a beginning of physical injury, pain arises and, like anxiety, acts as a warning signal. In extreme sexual behavior, in masochism, even fairly strong physical pain is not enough to cause the individual to abandon the sexual pleasure he gets from his passivity. Most psychoanalysts believe that pain is the goal of masochism. But perhaps the goal is sexual gratification that comes with physical injury, and the pain is no more than an unwelcome by-product.

Most passive wishes, when moderately indulged, are not dangerous. But there is a second great force behind the tendency to repress passive wishes, the force of pride. We are proud when we have or gain the attributes that society approves, and ashamed when we lack them. Feelings as universal and powerful as pride and shame must also have a biological function. In general, he who fills his social role successfully, feels proud. But pride is more directly connected with the exhibition of the sexual attributes that make one desirable as a sex partner. Either the attributes themselves are exhibited, or else some conventionally understood symbol of them, such as riches, clothing, children, or manner.

Since in the ultimate sexual act, coitus, the man is conventionally active and the woman passive, activity as a mode of behavior has come to be symbolic of masculinity, and passivity of femininity. Assumption of the active role is, therefore, a matter of pride with a man, and of the passive role a matter of pride with at least some women. Since men have passive wishes and women active ones, conflicts between wishes and sense of pride are inevitable. The fact that predominantly passive men and active women may nevertheless be proud of their behavior is the result of variations in the outcome of such conflicts. The outcome depends on the individual and on our clashing social standards. Its conditions and nature are of obvious importance, but it need not concern us further at this point.

To pursue our argument, the existence of any social group requires behavior of a passive pattern. Only leaders can be consistently active, and a stable society restricts leaders as well, and allows their authority to stem from their office alone and not from their personal wishes. Most of the members of a stable society must be obedient and accepting. Society has a number of instruments to encourage obedience and acceptance, and among these religion is especially useful. Religion attempts to substitute the virtue of humility for the shame of humiliation. It offers the reassurance that voluntary submission to divine will need cause no anxiety. However, in encouraging the passive instincts and their fantasies in order to stabilize society, religion tries not only to cancel anxiety and shame, the enemies of passive behavior, but it also uses—even encourages—guilt and despair. It does so by offering to substitute a sense of innocence for guilt and hope for despair.

Pessimism is not always available for use by religion. The spontaneous, minor depressions of daily life resolve of their own accord, while the major depressions of mental illness require more than religious ministration. In times of personal stress, religion has a greater appeal to the individual, and an effective religion is able to offer hope and extract submissive behavior at the same time. When the whole society is in desperate straits, the appeal of religion grows particularly strong, for it allows optimism instead of the pessimism that reason dictates, and it also acts to prevent the disorganization that panic breeds.

At times, religious prophets may attempt to create fear and despair, to turn the populace to religion. But it is guilt that religion uses most effectively to encourage passive behavior and ethical restraint. Guilt is an emotion that appears when active behavior has been carried beyond a certain point. The point at which the gratification of active instinctual wishes gives way to guilt is determined by constitutional and experiential factors, especially by the experiences of early childhood, and by the ethical principles taught by parents and other authorities. The effect of guilt is the ending of active behavior and its replacement by passivity. The passive acts include acceptance of punishment by authorities and of retribution by victims. In fact, guilt may be given as an excuse to justify the gratification of passive wishes. The child who is sexually stimulated by being beaten by his parent may misbehave to provoke a beating. Such strategies are more often employed among some adults than one might suppose. Guilt is one of the most powerful tools of religion, and where guilt is inadequate, religion may foster it by criticism, admonition, and indoctrination. By using this tool, religion can encourage the open gratification of passive wishes, especially those that serve the interests of the social organization. For this reason we shall now concern ourselves with the organ of conscious perception of guilt, the conscience, and with the origin and the dissipation of guilt.

THE SOURCES OF CONSCIENCE

Sometimes in the wake of war there comes an appalling breakdown of social authority. Looters roam about in streets gutted by fire, and ordinary men, who no longer feel themselves part of a community, try to sate the criminal impulses they have hitherto suppressed. The control that society exercises over its members is only tenuous.

It is easy to see the need for co-operation. In order to remain secure, everyone must refrain from aggressive acts against others. But there is no conscious, rational agreement or social contract. It is not the rational need for co-operation that is its impelling motive. What then is? No one has to pass laws to force people to get sexual gratification or to eat when hungry. The physiological reward, the pleasure of sex or food, is enough. There is also a very real pleasure in being accepted as a good citizen and a desirable friend, but the pleasure is a less urgent one. What is essential is the sense of obligation, which punishes and rewards internally. Without it the external authority of police, judges, and prisons, would fail. The law in the United States forbidding the sale or use of liquor could not be effectively enforced because people felt that it was not necessary to obey it.

The sense of social obligation, or the conscience, is not inborn (though the potentiality is). The earliest personal relationship the child appreciates is that with his parents, first of all with his mother. As she occupies herself with him, the child learns the pleasures of feeding, excretion, skin and, more particularly, genital contact, and exercise of his muscles. In the beginning he depends on his mother for many of these gratifications. Although, as he grows older, he is able to get some bodily pleasures apart from her, for a long time he remains dependent on his parents for security, food, shelter, and guidance. From his subjective point of view, the force that ties him to his parents is his love for them. The only catastrophes he can imagine are physical harm and parental rejection.

These misfortunes he learns to anticipate, and he becomes anxious and actively seeks his parents' love. He soon gets to know that he can keep their love only by restricting his personal pleasures. He must eat when and what the parents want him to. He must not handle his genitals. He must not empty the bladder or bowels except at specific times and places. He must put his toys away after he finishes playing with them, though he prefers to do something else. He must not beat his baby sister over the head when she grabs his toys. He must keep himself and his clothing clean. He must not demand affection when his parents are not inclined to give it. In general, he must restrict and defer his own pleasures because of what appear to him to be the arbitrary wishes of his father and mother.

As the child grows up, he tends to forget the particular circumstances under which he learned each restriction, for usually the learning was coupled with strong pain. The threat leads the child to an active forgetting of the whole experience to which it was attached. Yet the restrictions themselves stand firm, and by observing them he keeps his parents' love. Later, when the child becomes an adult, the restrictions form the basis of the conduct that ensures his acceptance by his social group. The efforts he made as a child to please the parents turn into the efforts to please the group.

This is a very rough description of the development of the conscience. The exact mechanisms of its growth are the subject of much controversy.

It would be a mistake to assume that the conscience is made up of a haphazard collection of restrictions and prohibitions. On the contrary, the child builds up in his mind and thereafter retains the image of an ideal person, who is the person his father and mother approve of completely. In technical parlance the image is called the *ego ideal*. The aggregate of rules for living implied by the ego ideal is referred to by psychoanalysts as the *superego*, which corresponds broadly to the conscience.[1] It is possible to distinguish between the two by using the word conscience for the moral rules of which one is aware, and the word superego for all the moral rules that guide conduct, many of which are not consciously known to the person who contains and obeys them. A man may be unusually scrupulous

---

[1] This is a simplified distinction, about which many psychoanalytic theorists have reservations.

in business without understanding basically why he is. If he is asked about his unusual scrupulousness, he may explain it by referring to moral or religious principles that he accepts, though he does not know it, in unconscious imitation of his father. The so-called "robber barons," who built great railroads and fortunes in the earlier periods of American history regarded their unscrupulousness as necessary and therefore justifiable. On the other hand, they often gave great sums to charity, but regarded their charitableness as only an indication of their good hearts. It seems reasonable to suppose that despite their protestations they suffered from an inner guilt, of which they were not consciously aware, and for which they atoned by the sacrifice of money.

The Sources of Guilt

The superego or conscience, then, has the job of enforcing rules of behavior. Usually the operation of the superego is silent, and one is not aware that there are desires being excluded from consciousness or allowed to appear only in disguised form.

For example, we know soft-spoken, polite, and sometimes obsequious people. They seem both to themselves and others to be wholly mild. It often happens, however, that when a person of this kind gets drunk or is provoked, he suddenly displays a viciousness of which no one, including himself, would have imagined him capable. A drunkard when sober is often unable to believe what he did when drunk. We may assume that the aggressiveness has been there all along, but that it has been repressed in the course of daily life. In fact, not only does the man hide the impulse by repression, but he may even appear to be dominated by particularly generous and pacific feelings.

The stronger the concealed aggressiveness, the more vig-orously it is defended against by an outward graciousness.

An adult with this personality may find himself asked to take care of a small child. Because the child is both helpless and often provoking, it may be hard for the adult to control himself. He may thereupon develop an uncom-fortable feeling of worry, or perhaps, anxiety.

Anxiety under such circumstances is usually neurotic, in the sense in which the terms anxiety neurosis and anxiety hysteria were used in the first chapter. The prob-lem of the nature and function of anxiety is one of the central problems of psychic disease, but since anxiety is irrelevant to the main theme of our argument, we shall not pursue the matter further here.

Suppose a relative of our hypothetical inwardly aggres-sive, outwardly benign person falls ill. The person is likely to experience a distressing sensation, which is identified as a feeling of guilt. If there is a good reason for the guilt, if some precaution has been neglected or if there is responsi-bility for an accident, the guilt is justified. This guilt is attributed to condemnation by his superego of what he has done. When, however, no objective reason can be made out why the individual should consider himself responsi-ble for the illness, his guilt is called neurotic and attributed not to anything he has done but rather to the condemna-tion by his superego of his unconscious hostile wishes. The guilt, therefore, is an instrument the superego uses to impose its requirements upon the ego, while the ego tries to avoid the superego's wrath, the guilt. The guilt is often accompanied by self-punishment, whether or not consciously appreciated. The guilt and self-punishment constitute aggression against oneself.

It was Freud's belief that there are two fundamental

types of energy available to the psyche. One, the source of erotic and co-operative activities, is constructive. The other is destructive, and is manifested in all disintegrating, hurtful, aggressive behavior. The destructive energy is turned against the outward world, but as is seen in guilt and self-punishment, it can be deflected by the individual against himself. He becomes both aggressor and victim, judge and prisoner, and, in suicide, even the executioner and the executed.

Guilt, in fact, is almost constant and almost universal. The drive for destruction, which gives rise to it, is plainly essential for achieving personal and social goals. We kill plants and animals to sustain us. It may be objected that killing an animal for human nourishment is hardly destructive, yet there are many people who are so impressed by the wrongfulness of the act that they refuse to eat meat. Murder is condoned and encouraged during warfare. But the aggressiveness implicit in even approved murder results in so much guilt that neurotic disturbances are caused in many soldiers.

Religion, which teaches that murder is forbidden, may nevertheless sanction killing in warfare. The permission is not always enough to dissipate all the guilt aroused. The Pima Indians were brave soldiers. They fought as allies of the United States against the Apaches. But although the Pimas praised the killing of an enemy above all other deeds, their usefulness as allies was greatly reduced by the law that the killing of an enemy must be expiated for a full sixteen days, during which it was forbidden to fight.

In daily life, aggression is expressed in quarrels, competition in school, business, and sports, and in political and religious rivalries. In each case the victory of one person necessarily results in the defeat of another, and we are

47

always supposed to feel sorry for the loser. There is nothing toward which society strives more constantly than the containment of destructive impulses.

Other activities that are a necessary part of normal social living breed guilt too. Saint Augustine makes the point that it is guilt that accounts for the secrecy attached to all sexual relations, proper as well as improper:

> Lust requires for its consummation darkness and secrecy; and this not only when unlawful intercourse is desired, but even such fornication as the earthly city has legalized. Where there is no fear of punishment, these permitted pleasures still shrink from the public eye. Even where provision is made for this lust, secrecy also is provided; and while lust found it easy to remove the prohibitions of law, shamelessness found it impossible to lay aside the veil of retirement. For even shameless men call this shameful; and though they love the pleasure, dare not display it. What! does not even conjugal intercourse, sanctioned as it is by law for the propagation of children, legitimate and honourable though it be, does it not seek retirement from every eye? Before the bridegroom fondles his bride, does he not exclude the attendants, and even the paranymphs, and such friends as the closest ties have admitted to the bridal chamber? The greatest master of Roman eloquence says, that all right actions wish to be set in the light, *i.e.* desire to be known. This right action, however, has such a desire to be known, that yet it blushes to be seen. Who does not know what passes between husband and wife that children may be born? Is it not for this purpose that wives are married with such ceremony? And yet, when this well-understood act is gone about for the procreation of children, not even the children themselves, who may already have

been born to them, are suffered to be witnesses. This right action seeks the light, in so far as it seeks to be known, but yet dreads being seen. And why so, if not because that which is by nature fitting and decent is so done as to be accompanied with a shame-begetting penalty of sin?[2]

Often people feel guilty because the demands of their bodies overcome or threaten to overcome moral proscriptions. There is tremendous moral pressure against masturbation, a widespread indulgence, and an enormous and almost universal guilt. Until recently even physicians considered masturbation to be a cause of mental illness.

In the course of a child's development he is forced, mostly by his parents, to accept a large number of restrictions, rules, and prohibitions. If one looks for it, it is not difficult to find evidence of strong resentment in children. Willful misbehavior, refusal to obey, and stubbornness, are dramatic displays of the strength of the resentment. But the approved mode of behavior is enforced by the superego, and by the time adulthood is reached there are few open signs of resentment against the parents.

The vigor of the moral control by the superego seems to have been derived from the early resentment of the child. In general, the more oppressive a child finds his parents' commands in childhood, the more vigilant he is in observing prohibitions as an adult. It is as though as an adult he were trying to treat himself as harshly as he would have liked to have treated his parents when a child. The old anger against them is turned against himself.

Another source of guilt lies not so much in revolt against superimposed behavior patterns as in uncertainty and conflict over the type of behavior that is demanded. The ego

[2] *The City of God,* translated by Marcus Dods, Book xiv, 18.

49

ideal is neither clear-cut nor static. There are two parents who have to be satisfied, each in different and sometimes antithetical ways. There are also playmates, teachers, and others endowed with authority, whom the child strives to please. The ego ideal is therefore a composite structure with some conflicting elements.

It is usual in our society for parents to teach their children absolute religious morality and yet to flout such obvious virtues as honesty, loyalty, trustworthiness, and respect for others. This makes it impossible for a child simultaneously to imitate his parents and obey them. Children are also confused by the activities that are reserved as the prerogative of adults. A boy of eleven who steals a smoke is imitating his father because he wants to be like him, but realizes that he is simultaneously rebelling against him. Inferior social groups usually have their codes of behavior set for them by superior groups, and the inferior are torn between their desire to identify themselves with their masters and to obey them. Negroes and Jews are assigned fixed, inferior social positions in a dominant white, Christian society. The individual Jew or Negro is then faced with the problem of whether he should complacently accept the role assigned to him or attempt to identify with the dominant group, by "passing" or competing. Whichever course is chosen, he feels guilty because one of his antithetical demands of conscience remains unsatisfied.

Difficulty in conforming to the ego ideal may arise in yet another way. Many boys grow up hoping to be like their fathers. However, as they approach the goal, they falter under the influence of guilt. Becoming like the father usually implies competing with him and—in a sense, therefore—displacing him. We know that in the families of successful men it is expected that the sons will take over the father's business or his professional practice. Yet it often happens that the son will reject the chance for easy success, despite adequate ability. If he comes under analysis, it may be found that the difficulty arises from a reluctance to compete with the father, a reluctance of which the son is not consciously aware. It must also be remembered that in his relationship with women the son is likely to assume the ideals of his father. There was a great deal of public revulsion at Freud's discussion of the Oedipus Complex, that is, of the son's sexual interest in his mother. The idea, however, is expressed quite boldly in the folk song, "I want a gal just like the gal who married dear old dad." In this sense, success with women also constitutes a competition with and displacement of the father and is often a source of guilt.

It is commonly taught that the wages of sin are misfortune. Although the purpose of the teaching is to discourage sin, it sometimes has a paradoxical effect. The occurrence of misfortune to those who are so indoctrinated convinces them that they have sinned and they become oppressed with guilt. When a tempest broke upon the ship in which Jonah was sailing to Tarshish, the mariners said, "Come and let us cast lots that we may know for whose cause this evil is upon us." There has been a continuous tendency among the Jews to attribute their misfortunes to their sins rather than to the wickedness of their oppressors. A Jewish prayer runs: "Because of our sins we were exiled from our land and banished from our territory. . . . and we are therefore not able to fulfill our obligations in Thy chosen house." It is interesting that with the re-establishment of the Jewish state a remarkable change in attitude has taken place. The self-deprecating, humble, almost broken people have become transformed into a proud, erect, and optimistic group, as though by reversing their previous misfortune they had simultaneously relieved themselves of a heavy burden of guilt. Among the ancient Greeks, there was also this retrospective sense of sin. Misfortune was to them a demonstration that it had been preceded by *hybris*, excess, arrogance, boastful self-sufficiency. According to the Far Eastern doctrine of *karma*, misfortunes in life are payment for evil deeds in a previous life:

> Those who are of pleasant conduct here—the prospect is, indeed, that they will enter a pleasant womb [that of a member of an upper caste]. But those who are of stinking conduct here—the prospect is, indeed, that they will enter a stinking womb, either the womb of a dog, or the womb of a swine, or the womb of an outcast.[3]

A Buddhist scripture says:

> There is the case of a person, a woman or a man, who takes life, cruel with blood-stained hands, given to striking and killing, and without mercy to living things. When that karma is worked out and completed, with the dissolution of the body after death, he is reborn in a state of misery, in an unhappy destiny, in a state of punishment, or in hell; or if he is not thus reborn, but attains the state of man, wherever he is reborn he is short-lived.[4]

In much the same vein, a talmudic rabbi claimed that a disease that made the breath short was the fitting punishment for slander.

---

[3] *Chandogya Upanishad,* 5, 10, 7. R. E. Hume, *The Thirteen Principal Upanishads,* Oxford University Press, 1931 (2nd ed.), p. 233.
[4] E. J. Thomas, *Early Buddhist Scriptures,* London, 1935, pp. 127-28.

CHAPTER 4

The Mechanisms for Dissipating Guilt

THE human psyche has many methods for dissipating the guilt that might otherwise become intolerable. Some methods are predominantly constructive, some destructive, and most, perhaps, a combination of both qualities.

Reparation is clearly constructive. If you were to break someone's lamp, you would probably offer to pay for it. Thereupon your mortification would turn to ease, your host's anger (if he were no more than an ordinarily irascible fellow) to calm, and the relation between him and yourself from strain to peace.

A more subtle form of reparation is psychic generosity to a person one has offended. A harsh word escapes you, and you become unusually polite, you hit a child in anger and then fondle it. And just as you may become irritated and vent your anger on a person who is not the cause of it, so your reparation may be indirect, that is, harshness against one man may inspire a reparatory kindness toward others. It is not surprising to find, for example, that Hitler, who was responsible for the destruction of more human lives than any other man in modern times, was an antivivisectionist and vegetarian. He considered himself a protector of children and animals.

Punishment is the destructive opposite of reparation,

though both motives sometimes operate together. To pay a tooth for a tooth is punishment in the outward guise of reparation. It is punishment because the loss of a tooth does nothing to replace the one that was lost before. The obvious constructive step was taken in Jewish law before long, and the principle was interpreted not literally, but as a demand for repayment in money of the value of the injury.

The desire to be punished shows itself in many ways. It is characteristic that during the depression that follows a relative's death, the survivors feel guilt and, often unknown to themselves, demand punishment. Some psychotics demonstrate this demand openly. A psychotically depressed individual may feel that he carries dangerous disease germs with which he infects his whole family. He will ask for punishment, even execution, because of his guilt. Most usually, the person who suffers from guilt feels much better either after he has been punished explicitly for his conduct, or after he has met with trouble, which is psychic if not legal punishment. "Take me up and cast me forth into the sea," said Jonah. "So shall the sea be calm unto you; for I know that for my sake this great tempest is upon you." And so the guilty person may look for punishment and await discomfort and even catastrophe with a measure of satisfaction:

> I am the man that hath seen affliction by the rod of his wrath. My flesh and my skin hath he made old: he hath broken my bones. My strength and my hope is perished from the Lord: Remembering mine affliction and my misery, the wormwood and the gall. This I recall to my mind, therefore have I hope.[1]

[1] *Lamentations*, iii.

Confession is still another means for dissipating guilt. "Leave not a fault unconfessed," a Buddhist scripture advises. The child keeps the secret of his trespass within him as long as he can, till he pours it out to his mother and feels relieved. Perhaps an element of reparation is involved, because the confiding child acknowledges the love and superiority of his mother. To be chosen as a confidant is usually to be praised.

The Buddhist may confess not alone his present sins, but the sins of his previous lives as well:

> Whatsoever be the sin that I, poor brute, in my beginning round of past births or in this birth have in my madness done or made others do or approved for my own undoing, I confess the transgression thereof, and am stricken with remorse. Whatsoever wrong I have done by sin against the Three Gems [the Buddha, the Law, and the Congregation of the Sons of Enlightenment, the monks] or father or mother or other elders by deed, word, or thought, whatever dire offence has been wrought by me, a sinner foul with many a stain, O Masters, I confess all. . . . The many whom I love or love not pass away while I stand here; only the dire sin wrought for their sake remains before me.[2]

Confession also has its communal aspects. Famine, to the Eskimos, was a sign that a taboo had been violated. They searched until they believed they had discovered the violator. If he confessed, the seals were supposed to become more amenable to being caught, but if he insisted on his innocence, only his death could smooth matters over. The confessions of a Jew tend to be communal. On the Day of

[2] Santi-deva (7th century or earlier), *The Path of Light*, abridged and translated by L. D. Barnett, London, 1947 (1st ed., 1909), pp. 41-42.

Atonement, the most sacred of his holidays, the Jew asks forgiveness for a whole long list of sins. But always it is for "the sin wherein *we* have sinned," so that the confession, by implicating everyone equally in his humanness, strengthens social ties, as does the fact that the confession is public and concerted.

Public confession has a contagious element with sometimes spectacular results. A United Press dispatch to the *New York Times* of February 10, 1950 told of a whole college that was suddenly seized by the contagious urge:

> A spontaneous mass confession by 1,500 students of Wheaton College passed the twenty-four-hour mark tonight and showed no sign of a let-up.
>
> All classes were suspended at the Liberal Arts School as the men and women students and their 150 teachers jammed into Pierce Memorial Chapel to proclaim their faith and confess their sins.
>
> Many students are training for religious life at the non-denominational college, which has a graduate theology school, but many others are liberal arts students.
>
> The demonstration has been going on since 7 P.M. last night when a few students went to the platform at a routine evangelical meeting to "testify" and the confessions developed into a mass movement.
>
> All last night and through today the students kept up a steady stream to the platform, leaving only occasionally to get a bite to eat or some sleep.
>
> Some were bold in their confessions, some hesitant and some tearful. One tall red-haired youth rose to say that he gave a diamond ring to his girl "that the Lord picked out for me."
>
> "But I had one difficulty in telling whether I

loved the girl or the Lord the most," he said. "Well, I got that straight with her this afternoon. The Lord comes first."

Almost all confessed wrongs against some person—their teachers, parents, friends or sweethearts—and named the offended party.

Now and then as the confessions went on the students called a halt, opened the windows to air the chapel and sang hymns until the admissions resumed.

Throughout the meeting the boys and girls sat together on the wooden seats of the chapel, dressed in sweaters, blue jeans and other conventional campus gear. Members of the football and basketball teams were among the confessors.

Authorities of the school, which was founded in 1860 and opened its doors to students of some thirty denominations, made no move to stop the demonstration.

"We will let it run its course," they said.

One girl said she had cheated even in Bible class. A music student confessed that she had been singing for her own pleasure rather than "the glory of God." Others said they had been guilty of cheating, lying and many other forms of wrong-doing.

But one girl went to the platform and said she thought her fellow-students were "silly to give testimony," because she hated insincerity and couldn't believe that all were sincere. Then she asked forgiveness for doubting their sincerity.

At times confession goes to a pathological extreme and becomes a symptom of disease rather than an effective method of relief. The blessed Pierre of Luxembourg began his devotions and austerities as a child. The son of a noble family, by the age of fifteen he had already been made

57

the bishop of Metz, and at his death at eighteen, in 1387,
he was a cardinal.

> Imagine, amidst the unbridled luxury of the
> courts of Berry and Burgundy, this sickly boy,
> horribly dirty and covered with vermin, as the
> witnesses attest. He is ever occupied with his sins
> and notes them down every day in a pocket-book.
> If he is prevented from doing this by a journey
> or some other reason, he makes up for this neglect
> by writing for hours. At night he is seen writing
> up or reading his pocket-books by the light of a
> candle. He rises at midnight and awakens the
> chaplains in order to confess; sometimes he
> knocks in vain—they turn a deaf ear to his noc-
> turnal call. If he obtains a hearing, he reads out
> his lists of sins from his little scraps. Towards the
> end of his life, he is shriven twice a day and will
> not allow his confessor to leave him for a mo-
> ment. After his death a whole chest was found
> filled with these little lists of sins.[3]

Confession and apology have the air of self-humiliation,
especially when they are so exaggerated. Self-humiliation,
however, takes nonverbal forms too. The case of a four-
teenth-century Hasid, a pious Jew, has many analogues
In the words of him who repeated the account:

> I have heard tell of a Hasid in Germany, who
> was not a scholar but a simple and honest man,
> that he once washed away the ink from a strip of
> parchment on which were written prayers which
> included the name of God. When he learned that
> he had sinned against the honor of God's name,
> he said: I have despised God's honor, therefore
> I shall not think higher of my own. What did he
> do? Every day during the hour of prayer, when
> the congregation entered and left the synagogue,

[3] J. Huizinga, *The Waning of the Middle Ages*, London, 1924, p. 168.

he lay down on the doorstep and old and young passed over him; and if one trod on him, whether deliberately or by accident, he rejoiced and thanked God. Thus he did for a whole year, taking as his guide the saying of the Mishnah: "The wicked will be judged in hell for twelve months."[4]

Religion often calls for self-abasement. To be greatest in the kingdom of heaven, says the New Testament, one must humble himself as a little child. And elsewhere it adds that each, in lowliness of mind, should esteem others as better than himself. The Psalms contrast the wicked with the meek. The Taoists, Chinese mystics, believed that the only useful quality was "weakness," that the sage was as submissive as the fool was brave, bold, and ostentatious. Sociological pressures may lie behind such self-abasement and philosophical arguments support it, but none of these would be effective if the humiliation were not able to give relief from the burden of guilt.

Self-denial is a method of easing guilt by blocking pleasure. Charity may be a sort of impersonal reparation to society at large, but it is also self-denial, as is fasting on holidays, or, to change the character of the case, joining the army because one feels guilty during wartime in living the life of relative ease of a civilian. As a Moslem mystic would put it, to have a full heart you must have an empty hand:

Do you know what poverty really is? If you have no knowledge of it, I will teach you concerning it. A faqir, although he possesses no treasure save the patched robe which he wears, conducts himself before men as if he had abundance. Though he be hungry, he boasts of satiety: for

[4] Quoted in G. G. Scholem, *Major Trends in Jewish Mysticism*, New York, 1946, p. 106.

his enemies he has nothing but friendship. He appears to be lean, wretched, and infirm, yet, in the matter of religious devotion, he is no whit behind the most robust and vigorous. Since his heart is full, though his hand be empty, he is able to weigh down the scales. Abandon yourself, then, to become one of the poor, so that the Almighty may take you under His care. He who is found in the company of those who are poor for the sake of God will be admitted into the palace of Eternity.[5]

To the traditional Hindu, the aim is quiescence and renunciation, to Saint Jerome it was a terrible struggle to subdue lust:

> Oh, how often, when I was living in the desert, in that lonely waste, how often did I fancy myself surrounded by the pleasures of Rome! I used to sit alone; for I was filled with bitterness. My unkempt limbs were covered in shapeless sackcloth; my skin through long neglect had become as rough and black as an Ethiopian's. Tears and groans were every day my portion; and if sleep ever overcame my resistance and fell upon my eyes, I bruised my restless bones against the naked earth. Of food and drink I will not speak. Hermits have nothing but cold water even when they are sick, and for them it is sinful luxury to partake of cooked dishes. But though in my fear of hell I had condemned myself to this prison-house, where my only companions were scorpions and wild beasts, I often found myself surrounded by bands of dancing girls. My face was pale with fasting; but though my limbs were cold as ice my mind was burning with desire, and the fires of

[5] *The Persian Mystics: 'Attar,* translated by Margaret Smith, London, 1932, pp. 86-87.

> lust kept bubbling up before me when my flesh
> was as good as dead.[6]

In subduing his senses and his guilt, St. Jerome, like St.
Augustine, seems to have kept his senses constantly hungry
through deprivation of their natural sustenance, and so to
have kept up a reciprocal, paradoxical-seeming "lust" and
guilt, at least temporarily aggravated by the procedure
designed to kill them. Conscious and unconscious guilt,
in other words, required that "lust" be subdued so as to
keep it psychically active, for self-denial is exerted to the
utmost when pulled to the highest possible tension. St.
Jerome could not succeed without failing or fail without
succeeding.

St. Jerome's self-denial lies on the verge of self-punishment, which is more severe. Drastic self-sacrifice may be
another form of self-punishment. Criminals who submit
to medical experiments are making reparation, denying
themselves some of the normal sensory pleasures, and
punishing themselves. People who are physically normal
but who fall into accident after accident in an uncannily
prolonged series are probably, with an unconscious de-
liberation, trying to hurt themselves so as to get rid of the
sense of having transgressed. They are the ones (not the
only ones, of course) who will run across a street against
the light and in full traffic, or across an icy pavement
inviting a broken leg, and who will court an amputated
finger by exposing themselves carelessly before a dangerous
machine. Suicide is, at least in part, the culmination of
urges to self-punishment in those who are pathologically
depressed. Pathological depression is often relieved by
serious physical injury, and it is supposed by some that

[6] F. A. Wright, *Select Letters of St. Jerome,* Loeb Classical Library,
1933, pp. 67-69.

success in self-punishment is one of the causes for the relief.

Self-punishment can go to unbelievably bloody extremes. To show how far it ventures and is sometimes applauded, we cite a description of practices still indulged in by Hindus during the early nineteenth century:

It is not uncommon to hear of Hindus, in case of a serious illness or of some imminent danger, making a vow to mortify some important part of their bodies, on condition of recovery. The most common penance of this sort consists in stamping upon the shoulders, chest, and other parts of the body, with a red-hot iron, the marks symbolical of their gods—brandings which are never effaced, and which they display with as much ostentation as a warrior does the wounds he has received in battle.

Devotees are often seen stretched at full length on the ground and rolling in that posture all round the temples, or, during solemn processions, before the cars which carry the idols. It is a remarkable sight to see a crowd of fanatics rolling in this manner, quite regardless of stones, thorns, and other obstacles. Others, inspired by extreme fanaticism, voluntarily throw themselves down to be crushed under the wheels of the car on which the idol is borne. And the crowds that witness these acts of madness, far from preventing them, applaud them heartily and regard them as the very acme of devotion.

Chidi-mari is another torture to which devotees submit themselves in honour of the goddess Mari-amma, one of the most evil-minded and bloodthirsty of all the deities of India. At many of the temples consecrated to this cruel goddess there is a sort of gibbet erected opposite the door. At the extremity of the crosspiece, or arm, a pulley is suspended, through which a cord passes with a hook at the end. The man who has made a vow to undergo this cruel penance places himself under the gibbet, and a priest then beats the fleshy part of the back until it is quite benumbed. After that the hook is fixed in the flesh thus prepared, and in this way the unhappy wretch is raised in the air. While suspended he is careful not to show any sign of pain; indeed he continues to laugh, jest, and gesticulate like a buffoon in order to amuse the spectators, who applaud and shout with laughter. After swinging in the air for the prescribed time the victim is let down again, and, as soon as his wounds are dressed, he returns home in triumph.

Another kind of torture consists in piercing both cheeks and passing a wire of silver or some other metal through the two jaws between the teeth. Thus bridled, the mouth cannot be opened without acute pain. Many fanatics have been known to travel a distance of twenty miles with their jaws thus maimed, and remain several days in this state, taking only liquid nourishment, or some clear broth poured into the mouth. I have seen whole companies of them, men and women, condemned by their self-inflicted torture to enforced silence, going on a pilgrimage to some temple where this form of penance is especially recommended. There are others, again, who pierce their nostrils or the skin of their throats in the same way.[7]

The thirteenth-century German mystic, Suso, wrote an autobiography in the third person, describing the radical means he used to mortify his flesh:

He was in his youth of a temperament full of fire and life; and when this began to make itself

[7] Abbe J. A. Dubois, *Hindu Manners, Customs and Ceremonies,* Oxford University Press, 1906.

felt, it was very grievous to him; and he sought by many devices how he might bring his body into subjection. He wore for a long time a hair shirt and an iron chain, until the blood ran from him, so that he was obliged to leave them off. He secretly caused an undergarment to be made for him; and in the undergarment he had strips of leather fixed, into which a hundred and fifty brass nails, pointed and filed sharp, were driven, and the points of the nails were always turned towards the flesh. He had this garment made very tight, and so arranged as to go round him and fasten in front, in order that it might fit the closer to his body, and the pointed nails might be driven into his flesh; and it was high enough to reach upwards to his navel. In this he used to sleep at night. Now in summer, when it was hot, and he was very tired and ill from his journeyings, or when he held the office of lecturer, he would sometimes, as he lay thus in bonds, and oppressed with toil, and tormented also by noxious insects, cry aloud and twist round and round in agony, as a worm does when run through with a pointed needle.[8]

Needless to say, these instances are extremes, yet at their root they are like the more amusing instances in which a small child will turn on himself, repeat in a mimicking voice, "Bad boy, mustn't do!" and spank himself as well as he can accomplish the awkward task. The theories according to which the exclusive goal of human beings is pleasure are clearly wrong. At least they are wrong if they do not recognize that we may hurt ourselves out of psychic necessity.

[8] *The Life of the Blessed Henry Suso, by Himself,* translated by T. F. Knox, London, 1865. Quoted by William James in *Varieties of Religious Experience,* Modern Library ed., p. 301.

One of the most common methods for dissipating guilt is rationalization. This is basically the unconscious substitution of specious, socially acceptable reasons for our acts, which appear in a less flattering light when described objectively. The doctor whose patient dies under his treatment feels comforted when he says to himself that the patient would have died soon anyway, or that some other doctor would have been just as likely to fail. Those who patronize black markets justify themselves by saying that if they do not, someone else will. People who profess only the highest motives justify their immoral conduct with the statement that, since society is rotten, there is no point in trying to act decently. They imply that they themselves are good at heart, but that a wicked society compels them to become unethical. Of course, there is some truth to such claims: if they were utterly baseless they could not serve as plausible excuses. The same is true of the argument of the criminal who exaggerates a valid point when he insists that illegal robbery is no worse than the everyday legal cheating and exploitation that is characteristic of our competitive society. The criminal's excuse contains the germ of self-criticism that sometimes makes rationalization a useful activity. Many doctors look on every unfortunate outcome as a chance for learning. When they describe an unusual death in a medical journal they are in a sense making a formal confession and humiliating themselves by a demonstrated failure, and also making a retribution that rests on a rationalization, as if they were glad of failures, which give them the chance to increase medical knowledge.

Closely allied with rationalization is the method of projection, which is the assignment of one's own traits to someone else. It has been found that college students with little insight into themselves tend to attribute their own stinginess, obstinacy, disorderliness, or bashfulness, to others. That is, the person who is obstinate tends to excuse himself by seeing others in his own image, though more often than not he cannot recognize himself in that same image. Children who lend a toy reluctantly feel guilty at their stinginess and tend to consider other children stingier than they would under other circumstances. Macbeth saw a murderer in everyone else, when the murderer was himself. We always blame the old Adam in us, Adam blames Eve, Eve blames the serpent, and the serpent blames God. Adolf Hitler blamed the Jews. In the testament he wrote just before his death he said that the Jews had provoked war:

> It is untrue that I, or anybody else in Germany, wanted war in 1939. It was wanted and provoked exclusively by those international politicians who either came of Jewish stock or worked for Jewish interests. After all my efforts of disarmament, posterity cannot place the responsibility for this war on me.[9]

So far the mechanisms for the dissipation of guilt that we have spoken of have been, on the whole, the necessary mechanisms of everyday life. But there are pathological forms we have not mentioned, typical of neuroses and psychoses in which guilt plays a role. Sometimes even physical symptoms may be produced by pathological guilt. Vomiting and nausea are frequently expressions of guilt based on aggressive childhood fantasies of biting and incorporation. Fantasies of this kind are reinforced by children's stories of animals that eat other animals, witches that eat children, and so on. The undoing of these guilt-

[9] H. R. Trevor-Roper, *The Last Days of Hitler*, New York, 1947, p. 177.

arousing impulses comes through vomiting, as though the impulses were a poison that had to be ejected.

Those mechanisms for the dissipation of guilt which result in self-injury rather than in a more disciplined acceptance of social restriction and authority, though evoked in the name of religion, represent a perversion of the function of guilt and, more often than not, represent modes of gratification of individualistic passive and reflexive instinctual wishes. But our main concern is not with pathology, but rather with guilt as it arises and expresses itself in normal life, and it is to a further examination of such guilt that we now turn.

CHAPTER 5

The Psychic Function of Religion

As WE have said before, the earliest social demands on the individual are those made by his parents. The parents seem to be actual psychic organs of the child. His psychically incorporated father and mother judge and punish and reward him just as the external ones do. The child's anger against their restrictions turns, as we have said, against himself and becomes the energy of the punitive aggressiveness of the inward parents. And, similarly, one may suppose that the superego's ability to bestow pleasure is derived from the pleasure felt by the child as a result of his parents' approval. The reward his conscience gives him is the residue of patting, kissing, smiling, and dandling, of the good taste of his mother's milk, and the feel of the powder she dusts on his chafed limbs. These are the primitive pleasures for which a baby strives, and it is their coalescence and attachment to obedience that give pleasure to an adult whenever he obeys his superego.

The experiences of early life create the most coercive, impulsive, and lasting elements of the superego. Yet they are kept secreted at a level where consciousness can hardly touch them. Consciousness and understanding are allied with the ability, resting chiefly on language, to organize experiences into patterns. The very young baby has no language and only the most elementary analogue to rational thinking, and therefore the adult consciousness, which is organized in verbal forms, finds it hard to recover the earliest events of life. Besides, the baby, being unable to think clearly, cannot distinguish between a prohibition and the terrifying threat attached to it, and excludes from his conscious mind threat and prohibition alike, retaining only, throughout all his years, an apparently inborn aversion to the prohibited act.

Parents can be terrifying to little children. Although the children are not able to formulate the intellectual proposition, their parents seem to them omnipotent, and alternately gracious and unbearably painful. The childish wish that provokes such overwhelming, painful reprisals is itself soon buried in the unconscious. It is evident from watching children that they are curious about their parents' genitals and sexual relations. Yet most people, including, very probably, the readers of this book, are not able to remember their curiosity and are inclined to deny that they ever had it. The children's curiosity and the adults' denial of it show that the reticence imposed by parents causes the repression of the very desire, let alone of the prohibition and the threat.

But as children grow up, the omnipotence of their parents is discovered to be delusive. A famous German author, describing himself at the age of four, said:

> The child has in his life a period—rather a long one—during which he believes that the whole world depends on his parents, or at least upon his father. And so he asks his parents for fine weather just as he might ask for a toy. This period comes to an end when the child one day discovers, to his great surprise, that some events

are as unwelcome to his parents as they are to himself. With the ending of this period there vanishes a great part of the mystic charm which gathered about the sacred head of the father. It is at this same time that a man's true independence begins.

My own eyes were opened to this fact by a terrible storm, accompanied by a thunderclap and a flash of lightning. . . . The maid, as frightened as the tiniest of the children, stood erect, crying "God is angry!" Then she added, didactically, "It is because you are such bad children!" This cry, though it issued from a humble source, forced me to look beyond myself and those about me: it kindled in me the spark of religion.[1]

Even in the mind of the nurse, the misdeeds of children were associated with punitive terror. But the terror was no longer associated with the father. The children were at the age when mastery over language and reasoning is already quite appreciable. As intellectual mastery grows, it becomes increasingly possible to distinguish between a wish or violation that is really dangerous to oneself and one that is not dangerous. To break a traffic law is not so terrifying to an adult that he must repress the consciousness of it, or of the impulse to drive over the speed limit at times. The superego has also become augmented by the common verbalized rules, learned in Sunday School and elsewhere, against cheating and stealing. Friends teach that you have to be a good sport and accept an unfavorable decision without protest, associates teach business ethics (or some code that passes by that often incongruous name), the newspaper editorial discusses moral issues in politics, and the philosophy teacher examines the rational basis of

[1] Hebbel, quoted in P. Bovet, *The Child's Religion*, New York, 1928, pp. 35-36.

morality in general. All these changes of the superego and augmentations of its scope, the whole body of ideals and prohibitions learned in later life, are conscious and tend to remain so.

When one of the latter, thoroughly conscious prohibitions is violated, uneasiness and guilt follow. But the factors involved are understood. If it seems reasonable to make retribution, it is made, and the guilt vanishes. The policeman catches you speeding, you pay the fine and decide not to speed again—or, if your conscience has a different cast, not to speed where policemen may be lurking. Or you may decide that the prohibition itself is unreasonable, and though uneasiness may persist for a while, it eventually subsides. Many Jews have abandoned the dietary laws that regulated them as children. The broader society does not observe the laws, and some Jews can think of no reason why they must be observed. Even though the dietary habits were inculcated from early childhood, a rational grasp of the issue permits the superego itself to grow changed and permissive. The issue is settled in open court.

Contrast this open-court proceeding with the police-court proceeding followed by the unconscious mind, which draws on the various unconscious sources of guilt. The prohibition is not disclosed, nor is the violation. The person stands accused of a crime that is never named. He bears witness against himself, but he does not know of what he is guilty or why.

There is the instance, which we simplify, of the girl who has been taught by her parents, whether directly or by implication, to what point she may go in her sexual activity. Her desire is conscious, as are the rules she accepts and the results of breaking them. If she does decide to break them, she feels guilty. Either, then, she stops, or

71

she continues and the guilt is gradually dissipated as the rule is replaced by another. But what, if as is not unusual, having no scruples she knows of against kissing, she kisses a man and afterwards feels nauseated and vomits. Psychoanalysis usually discovers that nausea and vomiting are not only a neurotic defense against fantasies of oral aggression, but also against those of oral impregnation.

In cases of this sort, the heavy guilt of unknown origin is often given a name like "tension" by the sufferer, who has no conscious scruples and no reason, therefore, to call the guilt by its more accurate name. Not to recognize the guilt as such is still another defense against the submerged irritant.

In most areas of serious moral concern there is an overlapping and integration of conscious and unconscious scruples, of open desires and latent fantasies. This creates the greatest difficulties for reason, which may believe that it is following its own dictates but is in fact rationalizing an unconscious impulse. The girl who has decided how far to go may simply be justifying and reinforcing an old desire she no longer recognizes. The aim of the childhood and adult desires may be alike, but the adult desire is given added force by the hidden and persistent infantile urge. It is not surprising that adolescents have so hard a time in finding their peace; and not adolescents alone.

Accumulated guilt, which a person may think is no more than uneasiness, gives rise to depression and pessimism. But the guilt and the depression are not the same. Depression is an immobilizing tendency that follows severe injury. The injury may be physical, as when a limb is lost or disease becomes crippling; or it may be psychic, a terrible insult, a lost love, financial reverses, or a grave failure in social relations. Guilt tends to enter the depression. The loss which precipitated the depression may be interpreted as the gratification of an unconscious hostile wish. The lost limb implies dependence on others, which arouses conscious guilt, and helplessness against aggression, which arouses the guilt that takes misfortune as the sign of wickedness. The depression itself is a guilt-arousing misfortune. But at their extremes, the guilt and depression are opposed. The cripple who has lost a limb has an urge to learn to get along by himself, and to this end he must rise out of his lethargy. Guilt mobilizes him into action, the use of the guilt-dissipating mechanisms, while depression immobilizes him by making him feel that nothing is worth while.

Tolstoy wrote graphically about his own depression. He was, he said, completely fortunate from an external point of view. He had a good wife and children, a large, prosperous estate, and fame. He was strong enough to keep up with the peasants at mowing, and able mentally to work eight and ten hours at a stretch without trouble. And yet life had come to seem a stupid, spiteful joke:

> At first I experienced moments of perplexity and arrest of life, as though I did not know what to do or how to live; and I felt lost and became dejected. But this passed, and I went on living as before. Then these moments of perplexity began to recur oftener and oftener, and always in the same form. They were always expressed by the questions: What is it for? What does it lead to? . . . My life came to a standstill. I could breathe, eat, drink and sleep, and I could not help doing these things; but there was no life, for there were no wishes the fulfilment of which I could consider reasonable. . . . And it was then that I, a man favoured by fortune, hid a cord from myself lest I should hang myself from the crosspiece of the

> partition in my room where I undressed alone
> every evening, and I ceased to go out shooting
> with a gun lest I should be tempted by so easy
> a way of ending my life. I did not myself know
> what I wanted: I feared life, desired to escape
> from it, yet still hoped something of it.[2]

It is usual, perhaps because of the impulsions of a victorious guilt, for a person to attempt suicide as he begins to emerge from depression. At any rate, Tolstoy discovered answers to his questions, the unconscious guilt was expressed through conscious rationalization, and he spent the rest of his life ascetically, in good works and in preaching—and, significantly, in harsh conflict with his wife.

When a person is caught in so deep an unconscious guilt, a thorough psychoanalysis can disclose its sources. When the guilt and its sources are made conscious, it becomes possible to bring it under intellectual domination. But there is another method for the handling of guilt of unconscious origin. The method is not as efficient in individual cases, but it can be applied to the large mass of humanity, while analysis cannot. This other method is provided by religion.

Conceive for a moment of a method for dissipating unconscious guilt that takes advantage of some of the salient facts of human life. First of these is the fundamental uniformity in the desires and goals of different people. We need not doubt that there are individual differences, or that the groups called races or cultures may possibly have psychic characteristics that on the whole distinguish them from one another; but the more we learn,

[2] Leo Tolstoy, *A Confession, The Gospel in Brief, and What I Believe,* translated by Aylmer Maude, London, 1940 (Oxford World's Classics), pp. 15, 17, 18.

74

the more the picturesque surface distinctions grow shadowy, and the more similar the plastic young psyches appear to be.

The second of the salient facts is that, although specific sanctions and prohibitions may vary from culture to culture, the essential pattern of emotional relations between parent and child remains similar.

The third of the facts is that the relation of the psyche to reality (reality taken in a more or less naïve sense) is not automatic but determined during childhood. An infant is thought not to be able to distinguish between its own body and objects outside it, such as the mother's breasts, limbs, or entire person. The solidarity of the infant with the universe foreshadows the solidarity the mystic tries to achieve. But the infant learns that there are some things from which it can and others from which it cannot be separated, and it begins to build up the concept of a self opposed to a not-self. However, the limits of the self remain fluid for a long time, allowing the child to establish somewhat at its own convenience where it ends and the outside begins. Children try to manipulate blocks and toys in ways physically impossible. "I don't want the ball to roll off," the child cries in frustration, not understanding that the will alone cannot restrain the ball. To distinguish external reality from subjective feeling demands an effort from children. They enjoy nonsense stories and absurdities because these relax the tension of adjustment to reality and allow the will to play a momentary god that dominates nature with its whims.

Strictly intellectual understanding and stringent testing of reality are adult functions that lie on the surface of the personality. When psychic difficulties arise, there is a tendency to regress to the more primitive modes of thought,

75

as we know from psychoanalytic studies. To use an analogy, when we are in real trouble we run back home to mother and ask her to comfort us. To project, for instance, is to attribute our own feelings to others. Projection is a return to the period when the boundaries between the self and the not-self can be shifted at will. It appears in the distortions of dreams, and in waking life most often in the areas that are not easily susceptible to clear-cut intellectual grasp. It appears, naturally, when the emotions are heavily enlisted. At least while they quarrel, husband and wife are sure that the other is exclusively at fault. The tendency in its most benign and familiar form is simply wishful thinking, the person's belief that things are as he should like them to be.

In children uniformity of desire and parental conduct are combined with the readiness to distort reality, producing the child's typical balance between desire, conscience, and action. There is a being, God, and an institution, religion, that serve the adult as magnified parents who enter the conscience and punish and reward, helping to maintain the adult's typical balance between desire, morality, and action. For all the crises it may undergo, and for all its growth, psychic life is continuous and repetitive.

We know that children, as they grow older, are likely to transfer to God much of their fear and love of their parents. The writer, Hebbel, whose description of a child's loss of faith in his parents we have quoted, goes on:

> One night when the wind whistled loudly in the chimney and the rain beat vigorously on the roof, at the moment when I was being put to bed the petition learned by rote and said with the lips only was transformed abruptly into a really anxious prayer. Thus was broken the spiritual

bond which till then had linked me exclusively to my parents. And very soon I came to make complaints to God about my parents even, when I considered that they had behaved unjustly towards me.

The relation between God and the parents, especially the father, is not concealed. God is our father in heaven, with the mercy, anger, and omnipotence, of the earthly father, and even, to simple men, his lineaments in a grandiose transposition. While the Bible says that God made man in His own image, from the psychic point of view it should be said that man made God in the image of the superego, or that he made God in his father's image. In more than one tradition the honor paid one's parents was connected with the honor paid God:

Let not a man say to himself: "Seeing that my Father in heaven was the first cause of my life, therefore will I go and do the will of my Father in heaven, and leave the will of my father and mother." Hence, "Honour thy father and mother" (Exodus xx, 12), and also, "Honour the Lord from thy substance" (Proverbs iii, 9). And let not a man say, "Seeing that my father was the primary cause of my life, I will do the will of my father, and neglect the will of my mother," for it says, "Ye shall fear thy God" (Deuteronomy vi, 13). If a man curses his parents or strikes or wounds them, God, if one might so say, folds His feet under the throne of glory, and says, "I have made my honour equal to theirs [the same word, honour, is used of father, mother, and God], for all three of us are equal in respect of honour. Had I been beside that man, so would he have done to me. Rightly, then, have I done that I have not lived in the house of that man." Whoever seeks many days and wealth and possessions and life in this world, and long life in the world to come which has no end, let him do the will of his Father in heaven and of his earthly father and mother.[3]

Many religions have had goddesses, representing fertility, and the Jewish-Christian-Moslem God also has some of the characteristics of the mother. Like the mother, our God provides us with food. He is as merciful as a mother. In fact, the Hebrew word for mercy, repeated in the phrase, "The Lord of Mercy," is the plural of *womb*. The Lord, like the mother, is the creative source. As Jewish tradition puts it:

> It is written, "Ye shall reverence father and mother, Thou shalt reverence the Lord thy God." Thus the Scripture puts the reverence of parents side by side with the reverence of God. And so it does as regards cursing God and cursing parents (*Exodus* xxi, 17 and *Leviticus* xxiv, 15). And this is just because all three are partners in man's creation.[4]

God the Father is endowed with a father's anger, but the anger, to anyone who worships him intelligently, cannot be malevolent, and evil anger must be ascribed to another being, the Devil. The Devil is a composite of one's own tempting but forbidden impulses which, when they beguile us, justify our punishment in our eyes; and of our resentment against our father and God, projected onto the Devil, who is His antagonist though ultimately subjected to Him. For him who obeys God there is Paradise, equivalent to the love granted the obedient child; and for him who defies God and seduces himself by electing to accept the Devil's seductions, there is Hell, equivalent

[3] C. G. Montefiore and H. Loewe, *A Rabbinic Anthology*, London, 1938, p. 501.
[4] *Ibid.*, p. 503.

to the terror of a little child whose parents turn on him, and to the power of one's own resentment against the Father, resentment that enforces His ordinances against ourselves. The Devil, who has tempted us, also punishes us, therefore: we torture ourselves with our own carnal impulses and punish ourselves for transgression in our own psychic hell:

> Scorched by the terrible and fierce rays of the sun, creatures dwelling in hell always drop there. In it there is a beautiful forest covered with cool foliage. The leaves and fruits thereof. . . . consist of sword blades. There bark a million of powerful dogs, with large mouths, huge teeth and dreadful like tigers to look at. Beholding before them the forest covered with dews and shades, creatures afflicted with thirst rush towards it. Having their feet burned by the fire raging underneath, they, greatly afflicted, cry out, "O father, O mother."[5]

Our forbidden impulses are like a mirage. The pleasure they promise is never attained because guilt burns our feet, and then we call on our parents to help us, because we know them to have been ultimately beneficent. Their commandments, prohibitions, and punishments, and the words and hands with which they soothe our hurts, live on in us enlarged into the massive figures and regions that tradition has created out of the projected figments of countless minds.

The very pains of hell help to make the religious picture of the world a psychically familiar one, and to assure the final benignity of the universe. "Whom the Lord loveth he correcteth, even as a father the son in whom he takes pleasure."[6] God, the projected superego, encompasses us

[5] *The Murkandeya Purana,* edited by M. N. Dutt, Calcutta, 1896. In R. O. Ballou, *The Bible of the World,* New York, 1939, p. 131.
[6] *Proverbs,* iii, 12.

in his motherly mercy and guards us in his fatherly omnipotence. Religion, therefore, tends to make us optimistic. It also tends to make us happy, because it provides socially sanctioned methods for the dissipation of guilt, the sources of which it specifies according to its own rationale. It heals us through repentance, prayer, righteousness, and ritual. It localizes with literal inaccuracy but symbolic correctness the sources of unconscious guilt. By touching these sources in a prescribed manner, it relieves guilt. It also builds up the conscious superego to the plan of a uniform and socially desired system of ethics, which is the ethics of the parents, objectified, codified, and generalized for all the community:

> Do not ill-treat any widow or orphan. If you do ill-treat them, and they cry out to Me, I will hear their cry, and I will grow angry and kill you by the sword; then your wives shall be widows, and your children orphans.
>
> If you lend money to My people, to a poor person among you, you must not be like a creditor toward him; do not charge him interest. If you take your comrade's robe as a pledge, you must return it to him by sundown, because it is his only covering, the robe he covers his body with. In what will he sleep? And if he cries out to Me, I will hear, for I am merciful.
>
> Do not report idle hearsay; do not join hands with a wicked man by being a malicious witness. Do not follow the majority for evil purposes. Do not show a poor man favoritism in his lawsuit; and do not deny any of your poor men justice in their lawsuits. Do not take bribes, for bribery makes the seeing blind and perverts the case of the just.[7]

[7] *Exodus,* xxii, xxiii. Translated, with elisions, by B. Scharfstein.

Thus religion, utilizing guilt, makes us eager for the passive acceptance of communal obligations and restrictions which are necessary for a stable society.

But together with such restrictions there are others, the reason for which is not as evident. How is it that food taboos and animal sacrifice are set side by side with mercy to the weak and poor? The answer is that even the most arbitrary-seeming ritual helps to subject us to communal interests and thus to make us ethical, as the following chapter undertakes to explain.

CHAPTER 6

Ritual

EVERY last one of us is a reconstructed rebel. Society dedicates itself to the thwarting or regulation of those deep-set impulses that if unchecked would be ruinous to any social order. Of the instruments that society uses to maintain the community, ritual is one of the most important.

A ritual is a sort of custom carried out with attentive formality. Behind it lies the force of conscience, which demands that the act be repeated at its due time. It is unlike a conscious ethical principle in that its formal purpose is often unknown except to the clergy, and sometimes only to the more educated even among them. Many Jews recite Hebrew prayers and Christians Latin ones the meaning of which they know only in the vaguest way. Among primitive medicine men, knowledge of the significance of ritual may be a trade secret. When James Pratt made a trip in the 1920's through the countries in which Buddhism was dominant, he reached the conclusion, which he admitted he was stating in an exaggerated form, "that in China there are many who believe in Buddhism and a few who understand it; but those who believe in it don't understand it and those who understand it don't believe in it."[1] When he asked the young monk who received him in a well-

[1] J. B. Pratt, *The Pilgrimage of Buddhism*, New York, 1928, p. 682.

known Peking temple, the Fa Hua Ssu, about the Buddhas before whom he was burning incense, the monk knew almost nothing.

> Looking about for something easy [wrote Pratt] I asked him the meaning of the prayer "Namu O-mi-to Fo," which he, in common with nearly all Buddhist monks, repeats many hundred times a day. He responded that he didn't know. He only knew that it helped your heart to say it over and over when you were in trouble. This question concerning the meaning of Namu O-mi-to Fo I made a point of asking in many parts of the country, as a kind of intelligence test for the monks. Namu is from the Sanskrit *Namas*, meaning hail, or adoration to, and the whole phrase is a form of worship, praise, and prayer, by which one gives "adoration to Amida Buddha," or promises devotion or self-surrender to him. I found a good many monks who knew all about it and repeated it intelligently. But I should say that about fifty per cent of the monks I asked proved to be as ignorant as the young man in the Fa Hua Ssu.[2]

There is no need to multiply examples, because the general ignorance of ritual purposes is obvious. Certainly the thought of the purpose is often absent during performance of the ritual, which becomes apparently self-sufficient and self-justifying. Those who do attempt explanations are usually rationalizing, and this is no less true in the present than it has been in the past. Now that we know how disease is spread, partisans of the different religions stress the hygienic value of ceremonial cleanliness. A relatively large percentage of the inhabitants of the United States has become infected with trichinosis, which

[2] *Op. cit.,* pp. 331-32.

comes principally from pork, and observant Jews are inclined to say that the Jewish prohibition against the eating of pork originated as a wise hygienic defense against disease. But this can be only a partial and superficial explanation, and by no means applicable to ceremonial cleanliness and food taboos as a whole, such as those that forbid Jews to eat fish without scales, swarming insects, whatever crawls on its belly, or quadrupeds with paws (whose carcasses may not even be touched).

The Brahmins of India have devoted the most extreme attention to ceremonial cleanliness. Cloth bought from non-Brahmins and clothes washed by a washerman have to be put into water again. Brahmin earthenware once filled with water and even glanced at by an "unclean" person must be broken. A Brahmin doctor will feel the wrist of a low-caste (Sudra) patient only through a piece of silk. The touch of a dog pollutes a Brahmin and must be washed off. It is obligatory for a Brahmin to bathe at least once a day. He does not allow himself to drink water drawn by strangers. He is careful to keep clean during urination and defecation. But all this cleanliness is ceremonial rather than hygienic. The Ganges is sacred, and water drawn from it even by untouchables may be drunk by Brahmins. Decontamination of cotton or of earthen vessels may be carried out through dipping in liquid butter. A well defiled by the corpse of a dog may be purified by having cow's urine poured into it, and cow's dung is also supposed to have purifying properties. Finally, much of the water used for ceremonial cleansing is polluted from a medical point of view because of primitive disposal of sewage. In other words, simple hygienic aims could not possibly have been of paramount significance in the development of such customs, which no longer have the

84

same strong hold in India they once did. More light can be thrown on the subject by history and sociology, and by the psychic groundwork of ritual, which we are venturing to explain.

Ritual attaches itself to the basic activities and events of life, which are naturally those that affect the emotions most deeply—eating, drinking, intercourse, birth, and death. Ritual involves taboos, but is something more. It is not predominantly a direct prohibition, but a channeling of impulses. Freud pointed out the similarity between religious ritual and symptomatic compulsions. Both are repetitive and stereotyped. In both the symbolism is not well understood by the person who carries out the activity, and when some detail is omitted, worry and a sense of impending danger follow. Misfortune among primitives is often attributed to the improper carrying out of a ritual. *Leviticus* contains a host of moral principles, taboos, and ritual regulations. It promises that observance will be followed by seasonal rains and good harvest, peace in the land, victory over enemies, and fruitfulness. But disobedience, it threatens, will be followed by terror and the burning ague, defeat in war and domination by hated enemies, plagues, wild beasts, famine, and cannibalism. "And upon them that are left alive of you," it adds, "I will send a faintness into their hearts in the lands of their enemies; and the sound of a shaken leaf shall chase them; and they shall flee, as fleeing from a sword; and they shall fall when none pursueth."[3] That is to say, the survivors will be overcome not alone by the enemy, but also by a guilty terror, from both of which only confession can save them. The religious chroniclers of the Jews, Christians, and Moslems, adopted the threat and the promise made

[3] *Leviticus* xxvi, 36.

in *Leviticus* as the basic categories for the explanation of the course of history.

The likeness between the religious ritual and the compulsive symptom can be carried too far. The first is historically conditioned and social in nature, while the second is private. But both rest on similar psychic mechanisms, especially on unconscious symbolism, and recur in typical ways. Perhaps the relation between ritual and compulsion can best be stated as follows: Both religion and neurosis take advantage of the psychic tendency to form compulsions and obsessions, religion by creating ritual and prayer, and neurosis by creating symptoms. In other words, ritual is a device available to the psyche to insure proper performance of a given task. Among lower animals, ritual is employed in courtship, mating and nest building. Human technicians—for example, surgeons, and even psychoanalysts—cast their techniques into the form of ritual wherever possible to effect correct performance.

The connection between one and another content of the unconscious mind, between its memories, emotions, and impressions, is not rational. It is based on superficial similarities in form or sound, simple contiguity in time or space, or the like. In so far as the products of the unconscious mind appear in ritual, ritual does not follow the processes of logic. Together with the other emotionally determined forms of behavior, it is constructed on symbolic lines.

A psychic symbol is a perception that, unknown to the perceiver, represents an element of an unconscious fantasy by virtue of an irrational relation, of the kind we have mentioned. Obsessions and rituals are compromises that set symbolic conditions for the performance of activities desired and dreaded alike. The common rituals show evident signs of the compromises, some in order to curb aggressiveness against individuals, some to regulate sexual activity, and some to ensure a general subordination to the social group.

The most extreme form of aggression is killing. No society can possibly allow random killing, but more than one has given a limited sanction to killing in the form of ceremonially regulated human sacrifice, followed, like as not, by cannibalism. The Aztecs sacrificed humans to end one astronomical cycle and begin another, and lit a fire in the breast of the victim, as if a new life were feeding on the old. On the holiday in honor of the fire-god, they threw prisoners of war into the flames. The Tupinamba, an Indian tribe of Brazil, first abused their enemies of war and told them of the fate that lay in store for them. Then, sometimes for years, the prisoners became members of the tribe, substituting for men who had died. The time for the execution arrived, the great ceremony was begun, the executioner faced a captive, and they spoke to one another as follows:

"Is not your nation our enemy? And are not you yourself the one who killed and ate some of my relatives and friends?"

"Most emphatically I am that one. Indeed I am the most powerful person imaginable and brave to boot. Were I not tied up here I would soon fall upon you and yours and destroy and then devour you as I have so frequently in the past."

"Well that is over for you. Now it is you who are going to be killed, cut up, barbecued, and eaten by me and my relatives and friends."

"So be it. But my relative will soon avenge me."[4]

The prisoner was killed, his blood drunk, and his flesh roasted and eaten. But the executioner, to escape the avenging spirit of the dead man, fled wildly to his hut, while his female relatives rushed about calling out a new name that he was assuming. Then the executioner lay bound in his hammock for four days. Afterwards he remained there speaking to no one, abstaining from certain foods, and not setting foot to the ground. When his hair had reached the right length, there was a feast at which it was cut, and at which he took his new name and submitted to the cutting of scars into his thighs, legs, arms, and breast.

What is the psychic significance of human sacrifice and cannibalism of this kind? They may of course be speculatively related to Freud's belief that society plays out the primal drama of the killing of the father. But some meanings are evident without much speculation. The victim is made to say that he wants to kill and devour his captors. His words represent at least in part the projected desire of his captors to kill and eat him, a desire they express at once. But no sooner is the prisoner killed, than his executioner is stricken by fear and guilt. He is bound, he is not allowed to eat any of the dead man's flesh, nor any game or fish, and scars are cut into him. He and his group seem afraid of the murderous impulses that have momentarily been liberated. First they threaten the captive, then they allow him to live in peace as a member of the community, who may not be killed, then they threaten him again and kill and eat him, and then the killer avoids meat and mortifies himself. What is all this but cere-

[4] Quoted in Paul Radin, *Indians of South America*, New York, 1942, p. 103, from A. Métraux, *La Réligion des Tupinamba*, Paris, 1928.

monial containment of aggression by a limited surrender to it?[5]

The Semites practiced the sacrifice of children. Perhaps that is the original significance of the requirement in *Exodus* that the first-born children were Jehovah's. That, too, seems to be the significance of the intended sacrifice of Isaac. But afterwards the Jews redeemed their first-born with a payment, a symbolic representation, it may well be, of an act that had become in their eyes too horrible and too dangerous an incitement of the lust to kill. The consumption of blood is not permitted Bedouins or observant Jews. Life is believed to reside in the blood, and the guilt of killing is lessened if the blood is released. Orthodox Jews eat only *kosher* meat, the animal having been killed as painlessly as possible, by bleeding from a cut made by an extremely keen knife drawn across the throat. The slaughterer must know the laws of his trade and be morally and physically unblemished. What does such killing represent but an attempt to surround human aggressiveness with a wall of ceremony and mercy, without, however, abolishing its useful forms? And a similar reason, among others, can be given for food avoidances like those of the Navaho, who may not eat fish, or most water birds or animals, or raw meat, or even cut a melon with the point of a knife. The point of a knife is fearful and not to be lightly used. It is too tempting to an inwardly aggressive man. The symbol of a knife has more than one meaning, and killing is among them.

When an antivivisectionist accuses the doctors of cruelty, he is testifying that he feels that if he were to dissect animals it would be to gratify the cruel streak in his nature,

[5] Again we must stress that we do not think our explanation to be exclusive or complete.

which he projects onto the doctors; and when they carefully anesthetize the experimental animal, they testify to the desire to reduce pain and allow as little scope as possible to impulsive, as against rational killing. There are men in India who wear gauze over their mouths in order not to breathe in and injure even a tiny insect. So far do we ritualize and protect ourselves against our own aggressiveness by way of unconsciously symbolic acts.

Funeral rites reveal love for the deceased, guilt, and occasionally pleasure. When food is given to the dead, among primitives, or in ancient Egypt, or elsewhere, or when the custom is followed of naming someone to replace the dead person (reflected in our practice of naming a child after a grandparent) there is open reluctance to part with the loved one. That guilt should be felt at the killing of an enemy and his spirit feared follows from direct if unscientific reasoning. But why do primitives often fear the spirits of their own beloved relatives? Some American Indians went through ceremonies designed to cut the trail of the dead man and make forgetfulness fall on him, thus hindering him from coming back. The Iroquois believed that the dead would need weapons, but refused as a rule to place knives and tomahawks with a corpse, for its spirit might return with vengeance in mind and tomahawk in hand. Relatives particularly, among some Eskimos, for example, avoid the corpse.

Is the avoidance and fear of the dead merely an indication of a fear of dying? There seems to be something more: first, the sense of guilt that follows misfortune, and, secondly, a ritual recognition of one's own suppressed hostility toward the dead projected onto the dead in the form of their hostility toward the surviving relatives. Compulsive washing of the hands is, among other things, a sign of guilt. The murderer, Macbeth, felt his hands were always bloody, and our avoidance of the dead and fearful disgust at touching them may also bear the trace of a feeling of responsibility for their death, for there must have been times when we wished for it.

If it were not true that we entertain at least unconscious hostility toward friends and relatives, it would be hard to explain funeral rites that combine mourning with undisguised pleasure. A Chinese family may impoverish itself to pay for a funeral and mourn for a parent for more than two years, but the funeral itself is an occasion for what must be called merrymaking. Lin Yutang insists that he cannot distinguish between a Chinese funeral and wedding procession until he sees either the coffin or the wedding-chair.

The elaborate and picturesque death ritual of the Balinese culminates in a banquet, procession, and cremation, the elderly men sitting around drinking and boisterous, the others excited over the spectacle, but not mourning. During the procession the men turn the body in different directions to confuse it and keep it from returning to the house. At the burning, just as before, the corpse is poked and laughingly urged to burn faster, while the mob snatches away the finery in which the funeral towers are decked, all to the sound of orchestras and merriment. Forty-two days later the ashes are cast into the sea. The dead man is now consecrated to help the living, and the participants splash around happily in the waves. It can be said that because the Balinese believe in reincarnation, they have no reason to mourn, and the corpse is of no importance. But the very way in which the corpse is treated shows that it is important, and the object of fear and malevolence. The dead man is treated with an ambiguity of dislike and love in a ritual drama that expresses the unconsciously ambivalent feelings of the participants.

Rites of sacrifice and death are largely concerned with channeling the aggressive impulses, while puberty and marriage rites are more directly concerned with regulation of the sexual drive. Puberty rites often go with circumcision. Among the Aruntas of Australia, the boy who is becoming a man is both circumcised and painfully bitten on the head by the old men. The boy has been separated from the women, who become for him, for the first time as far as the community is concerned, properly sexual objects. That he is a sexually mature man is marked by the imparting to him of a religious secret no mere child or woman may know. A lecture on morality and a set of food taboos are part of the rites.

The long ceremonies have the purpose, as the natives recognize, of ensuring that the elders keep control in their hands, get the services of the young initiates and the food forbidden the latter, and enjoy the young women for themselves. But why the scarring and circumcision? The scarring does not make hair grow, as the Aruntas allege, nor does the circumcision have a conscious practical motive sufficient to explain it. The explanation is that sexual morality inculcated together with pain, pain most especially to the sexual organ, is highly effective. There seems also to be a renewal of the threat, which so terrifies very young boys that they suppress the memory of it, that misconduct will be punished by cutting off of the penis. Where this unconscious fear persists, as it apparently does in surprisingly many men, at least in our culture, circumcision confirms and reinforces the fear, making it the more difficult for the initiate to be merely promiscuous, that is, to disregard the communal restraints on sex. Among the Aruntas not only is the initiate into adulthood circumcised, but the whole urethra is split below to its middle in the sub-incision ceremony, making a wound that never closes. Among the tribes of South Africa that practice circumcision, an uncircumcised man never rises above the status of a boy. Women look down on him, and he is not allowed to marry or take part in councils.

Circumcision among Jews and Moslems has been a major sign of social unity. There is reason to believe that post-natal circumcision among Jews is a variant of puberal circumcision (at least Ishmael, who represents the "Arabs," was circumcised at thirteen, the age at which Jewish boys enter on the obligations of manhood). Jews are obliged to die rather than forego circumcision. The effort of the emperor Hadrian to forbid the practice helped cause a bitter revolt of the Jews against Rome in 132 A.D.

The ritual of Jewish circumcision does not have, or no longer has, an openly sexual character, but is consciously directed toward loyalty to God and Judaism. The circumciser prays:

> Blessed art Thou, Lord our God, King of the Universe, who didst sanctify the beloved (Israel) from birth, and impress the law in his flesh, and mark his descendants with the sign of holy covenant. In return for this, Eternal God, our Stronghold, order that our flesh-brotherhood be saved from destruction, for the sake of Thy covenant Thou didst impress in our flesh. Blessed art Thou, Lord, Maker of the Covenant.

The circumciser then recalls the passage in Ezekiel in which Jerusalem is compared to a newborn babe left weltering in its blood. God said, "Live through your blood, live through your blood." And God, according to Ezekiel's

metaphor, clothed Jerusalem in finery, decked her in orna-
ments, and guarded her and fed her; but she played the
harlot.

There is more than a hint here of a bond in the flesh
like that celebrated in totemic rites, or in human sacrifice.
The blood shed in circumcision *is* sacrificial, and through
it the child becomes a Jew and attains a greater life. There
is also, in Ezekiel's metaphor, the hint of a father's jealousy
for his daughter who leaves him for another's love. Jews
must circumcise the foreskins of their hearts, as the Hebrew
idiom puts it. Their sexual obedience, assuming this to
be the original meaning of the ceremony, must be extended into a total obedience to the ordinances of God,
and a total acceptance of practices the historic community
approves.

Confirmation services among Christians and Jews are
modern forms of puberty rites. It would take us too far
into anthropological detail to speak of other puberty rites
or of the innumerable varieties of marriage ceremonials.
Many of the latter are accompanied by sexual behavior
that is not allowed at other times, confirming the thesis
that ritual may permit at least symbolically the very act it
is meant to regulate. All of the ceremonials play up the
individual's obligations and confer freedom on him at the
price of obedience. He solemnly repeats the formulas that
define the bounds of his liberty, he pledges himself to remain in licit wedlock. The community may exact a high
price. In Jewish law, a husband was *required* to divorce
an adulterous wife, even against his will, and it was also
his duty to divorce a wife who had been barren for ten
years.

The almost universal prohibition of sexual congress
during and just before and after menstruation has a sym-

bolic, protective character. The religious laws regulating menstrual separation of the sexes are upheld by attitudes that are not ostensibly connected with religion. People say of intercourse during menstruation, "It's disgusting," or "It's unhygienic." To dispose of the latter argument first, although some physicians have tried to prove that menstruating women exude a poison, a "menotoxin," which is destructive to plants and animals alike, no adverse consequences of intercourse during menstruation are known to medicine. The argument that the practice is disgusting is merely another way of saying that an ingrained custom forbids it.

It becomes quite clear to the psychoanalyst that both men and women unconsciously identify menstrual bleeding with bleeding from a wound. Menstruation is frequently spoken of among women as "falling off the roof." Women under analysis often announce the advent of their menstrual period with dreams of a bleeding wound caused by violence, or by dreams of a bleeding sore.

That violence and aggression are of importance in the sex act is common knowledge. Although frank sadism such as flagellation is considered a perversion, many "normal" men increase their sexual pleasure by hurting women during coitus by increasing the vigor of sexual movement, and by biting, scratching, squeezing, and so on. Rape is not simply illegal intercourse, but violent intercourse often accompanied by murder.

If sexual violence is to be confined within socially desirable limits, it is obviously helpful to dissociate the sex act from the blood of menstruation. When, as may happen, sexual violence is condoned or encouraged, conditions are always attached. In the following passage from a Hindu scripture, the man about to violate a woman is first re-

95

quired to try to bribe her, and, if he fails, to repeat a formula during the violation:

> If she should not grant him his desire, he should bribe her. If she still does not grant him his desire, he should hit her with a stick or with his hand, and overcome her, saying: "With power, with glory I take away your glory!" Thus she becomes inglorious.

The same scripture enjoins a man to repeat an efficacious spell or formula during the sex act:

> The woman whom one may desire with the thought, "May she enjoy love with me!"—after inserting the member in her, joining mouth with mouth, and stroking her lap, he should mutter:—
> "Thou that from every limb art come,
> That from the heart art generate,
> Thou art the essence of the limbs!
> Distract this woman here in me,
> As if by poisoned arrow pierced!"[6]

Again there is the arrow, the pain, to increase the pleasure of sex, and always there is society trying to harness unruly impulses to its own more sedate chariot.

Prayer has the function of generally subordinating men to communal interests. If you may not partake of food without saying grace, the invisible community has prevented you from giving in unthinkingly to your hunger and has forced you to pause in its honor. The Zen Buddhists of Japan are living examples of how constrained, prayerful, and ceremonial eating may become, and how it

[6] R. E. Hume, *The Thirteen Principal Upanishads*, Oxford University Press, 1931 (revised ed.), p. 169.

may symbolize and establish the submission of the individual:

At meal-times a gong is struck, and the monks come out of the Meditation Hall in procession carrying their own bowls to the dining-room. The low tables are laid there all bare. They sit when the leader rings the bell. The bowls are set— which, by the way, are made of wood or paper and well lacquered. A set consists of four or five dishes, one inside the other. As they are arranging the dishes and the waiting monks go around to serve the soup and rice, the *Prajna-paramita-hridaya-sutra* is recited, followed by the "Five Meditations" on eating, which are: "First, of what worth am I? Whence is this offering? Secondly, accepting this offering, I must reflect on the deficiency of my virtue. Thirdly, to guard over my own heart, to keep myself away from faults such as covetousness, etc.—this is the essential thing. Fourthly, this food is taken as good medicine to keep the body in a healthy condition. Fifthly, to ensure spiritual attainment this food is accepted." After these "Meditations" they continue to think about the essence of Buddhism, "The first mouthful is to cut off all evils; the second mouthful is to practise every good; the third mouthful is to save all sentient beings so that everybody will finally attain to Buddhahood."

They are now ready to take up their chopsticks, but before they actually partake of the sumptuous dinner, the demons or spirits living somewhere in the triple world are remembered; and each monk taking out about seven grains from his own bowl, offers them to those unseen, saying, "O you, demons and other spiritual beings, I now offer this to you, and may this food fill up the ten quarters of the world and all the demons and other spiritual beings be fed therewith."

While eating quietude prevails. The dishes are handled noiselessly, no word is uttered, no conversation goes on. Eating is a serious affair with them. When a second bowl of rice is wanted, the monk folds his hands before him. The monk-waiter notices it, comes round with the rice receptacle called *ohachi*, and sits before the hungry one. The latter takes up his bowl and lightly passes his hand around the bottom before it is handed to the waiter. He means by this to take off whatever dirt that may have attached itself to the bowl and that is likely to soil the hand of the serving monk. While the bowl is filled, the eater keeps his hands folded. If he does not want so much, he gently rubs the hands against each other, which means, "Enough, thank you."

Nothing is to be left when the meal is finished. The monks eat up all that is served them, "gathering up of the fragments that remain." This is their religion. After a fourth helping of rice, the meal generally comes to an end. The leader claps the wooden blocks and the serving monks bring hot water. Each diner fills the largest bowl with it, and in it all the smaller dishes are neatly washed, and wiped with a piece of cloth which each monk carries. Now a wooden pail goes around to receive the slops (when the slop-basin goes around, spiritual beings are again remembered). Each monk gathers up his dishes and wraps them up once more, saying, "I have now finished eating, and my physical body is well nourished: I feel as if my will-power would shake the ten quarters of the world and dominate over the past, present, and future: turning both the cause and the effect over to the general welfare of all beings, may we all unfailingly gain in

98

powers miraculous!" The tables are now empty as before except those rice grains offered to the spiritual beings at the beginning of the meal. The wooden blocks are clapped, thanks are given, and the monks leave the room in orderly procession as they came in.[7]

Ritual prayer is a reminder of obligations and a persistent subordination to a social design.

My son [said a Winnebago Indian], when you grow up, see that you are of some benefit to your fellow men. There is only one way in which you can aid them, and that is by fasting. Our grandfather, the Fire, he who at all times stands in the centre of our dwelling, sends forth many kinds of blessings. Be sure that you make an attempt to obtain his. Remember to have our grandfathers, the war-chiefs who control war, bless you. . . . If you cannot obtain war-blessings, fast at least for a position in life. If you fast when you marry you will get along well. You will not have to worry about your having children and your life will be a happy one. Fast for the food you are to receive.[8]

The Winnebago was in effect exhorting his son to remember his ancestors, who formed the historic community, and to fast to gain the regard of the spirits, for in fasting he would curb his desire, counter his guilt, and remove himself the further from anarchic freedom.

In much the same vein, but with a clearer consciousness of ethics as we see it now, Buddhist laymen took eight

[7] D. T. Suzuki, *Essays in Zen Buddhism (First Series)*, London, 1949 (first ed. 1927), pp. 321-23.

[8] Paul Radin, *Crashing Thunder, The Autobiography of an American Indian*, New York, 1926, pp. 56ff. As quoted in P. Radin, *Primitive Religion*, New York, 1937, pp. 16-17.

fast-day vows: to lay aside the use of the stick or knife and shun the taking of the life of any creature; to accept and expect what is given, purely and without stealing; to practice continence, avoiding the village practice of sex intercourse, during the fast; to shun falsehood and speak truth; to shun the carelessness that resulted from strong drink; to eat only one meal during the fast day; to refrain from dancing, singing, music, garlands, scents, and unguents; and to avoid a bed, couch, or mat. For a short while the Buddhist layman was subjecting himself to the regimen of a monk. He was combining rational rules of conduct with self-denial, restraint from pleasure, conquest from desire, and surrender of the self to the community.

This, as we have repeated, is the aim of prayer, whether confessional, self-humiliation, declarations of God's glory, requests for God's assistance, or recitals of human obligation. The greatest submissiveness to God is human sacrifice. In Judaism, as the story of Isaac and the dedication of the first-born to God is believed by some to show, animal sacrifice was substituted, the animal remaining a symbol for the man. Still later the Jews substituted prayer for animal sacrifice, so that historically the submissiveness acknowledged in Jewish prayer may be a substitute for the total submission of life to a deity.

Ritual is to humans what the bit and reins are to the horse. Ritual uses group singing, dancing, prayer, and display, conscious moralizing and unconscious symbolism, tantalizing permission and painful threats, the whole mind and the whole body, to coalesce the individual into the group, which would be fragmented by his uncurbed impulses. Ritual, in other words, is a practical instrument of ethics. When effective it not only curbs, but also helps to create the desire to serve the community in an extension of the service that ritual calls for. When Rab Assi, a scholar of the time of the Talmud, was dying, he wept. He wept because, though he had abided by the laws, done kind deeds, and raised up disciples, he had never been willing to serve as a judge. His story ends: "A man who retires to his house and says, 'What have I to do with the burden of the community, or with their suits, why should I listen to their voice? Peace to thee, O my soul'—such a one destroys the world.[9]

[9] Montefiore and Loewe, *A Rabbinic Anthology*, p. 352.

CHAPTER 7

Religious Experience

CONVERSION

CONVERSION, like prophecy and mysticism, has too many forms to be discussed here fairly. But it is typical of conversion to be preceded by morbid feelings, which shade into the apathy of depression. These feelings are recurrent or prolonged until, one day, if the conversion is of the sudden kind, doubt, anxiety, internal strife, and despair, are replaced by sureness, serenity, peace, and optimism. As the revelatory experience grows more intense, the person may be moved to weep, cry out, shudder, fall to the ground convulsed, even to lose consciousness; and then it is as if a veil were torn away and the world transfigured in the light of a warm perception edged with ecstasy. Everything seems beautiful and good.

One of the most famous instances of conversion was that of Saint Augustine. Typically, he was a rebellious man. He had strong appetites and a strong, though at first somewhat latent conscience. In his *Confessions* he pays little attention to his father. Monnica, his mother, was a pious Christian, always teaching Augustine virtue, self-abnegation, and chastity. In his own eyes he was a deplorable child. It is true, probably, that his reminiscences of his childhood are strongly colored by his later doctrines of sin, but that the child felt guilt is made clear by his nagging remembrance of outwardly trivial episodes, such as the one in which, together with a gang of boys, he went one night to steal the fruit of a pear tree. The boys were not hungry. They flung most of the pears to the swine. The pleasure of the theft, so Augustine says, lay in the stealing.

Augustine's father, by then a Christian catechumen, had been glad at the signs that Augustine's sexuality was awakening, but when Monnica was told,

> she then started up with fear and trembling. . . . For she desired, and I remember privately warned me, with great solicitude, not to commit fornication; but above all things never to defile another man's wife. These appeared to me but womanish counsels, which I should blush to obey.[1]

Soon thereafter, at the age of seventeen, Augustine went to Carthage.

> To love [he says a little enigmatically] and to be loved was sweet to me, and all the more when I succeeded in enjoying the person I loved. I befouled, therefore, the spring of friendship with the filth of concupiscence, and I dimmed its lustre with the hell of lustfulness; and yet, foul and dishonorable as I was, I craved, through an excess of vanity, to be thought elegant and urbane [III, i].

A few years passed. He concerned himself with the doctrines of the Manicheans, which he found wanting. His father had died. His mother, although she had begun to

---

[1] Augustine, *Confessions*, translated by J. G. Pilkington, II, iii.

avoid him because, writes Augustine, she hated the blasphemies of his error (presumably in refusing Christianity), nevertheless allowed him to live with her. The reason was the good augury of a dream in which

> she saw herself standing on a certain wooden rule, and a bright youth advancing towards her, joyous and smiling upon her, whilst she was grieving and bowed down with sorrow. But he having inquired of her the cause of her sorrow and daily weeping (he wishing to teach, as is their wont, and not to be taught), and she answering that it was my perdition she was lamenting, he bade her rest contented, and told her to behold and see that where she was, there was I also. And when she looked she saw me standing near her on the same rule [III, xi].

Augustine became a teacher of rhetoric. His very dear friend died, and Augustine fell into a black state of mind; and when he asked himself why he sorrowed so, he could not answer. He left to return to Carthage, where the sorrow gradually subsided. In spite of his mother's wild grief, he later set out for Rome. From there he went to Milan, where his mother followed him, declaring that before she died she would see him a Christian. Slowly his opinions changed in the direction of Christianity. For thirteen years he had lived with a mistress, but Monnica succeeded in engaging him to a young girl. In two brief, moving sentences Augustine speaks of his loss:

> My mistress being torn from my side as an impediment to my marriage, my heart, which clung to her, was racked, and wounded, and bleeding. And she went back to Africa, making a vow unto Thee never to know another man, leaving with me my natural son by her [VI, xiv].

Since the girl that had been chosen was still two years too young for marriage and Augustine had not the strength to wait, he got another mistress, though the pain of separation from his former mistress grew more rather than less desperate. Augustine was now thirty years old, and wretched. In his thirty-second year he was converted to Christianity.

Augustine's early life was thus full of psychic conflicts. It is difficult to learn just what his early relations with his parents were. He stole food from them. This may have been an attempt to recapture maternal love. Food stands for maternal love because it is the chief gift of the mother and is from earliest infancy always associated with her. He considered the maternal love to have been denied him. "My parents," Augustine recalls, "seemed to be amused by the torments inflicted upon me as a boy by my masters" (I, ix). His later promiscuity, assuming it was unusual in his milieu, may have been a forceful effort to re-establish a close relationship with his mother on his own terms, that is, by taking rather than waiting expectantly. But Monnica, his conscience, would not let him go. The dream into which she projected her hope of winning him impressed itself on his mind. The death of his friend was a new source of guilt. And Monnica admonished, pleaded, and wept. Augustine was wretched; and then he was converted.

Conversion is the end, at least temporary, of a powerful struggle among psychic impulses. Resistance on one side breaks down, though often only when the battle has reached a climactic stage. Augustine reached this stage at the time of his supreme misery (the description is his own), after he had heard an impressive account of the life of Christian monks. Augustine lashed his soul, but it would not obey, for it was still in rebellion. He went into the garden of the house, followed by his friend, Alypius, who could see that he was badly troubled. Augustine tore his hair, struck his forehead, entwined his fingers and clasped his knee, wondering all the while that his will could so move his body and yet not move the soul to accomplish its greatest will. The lashes of fear and shame were redoubled. He came to the resolve, he was about to accomplish it, he drew back. The chaste dignity of Continence appeared before him and extended her holy hands to embrace him. She seemed to say, "Shut up thine ears against those unclean members of thine upon the earth, that they may be mortified. They tell thee of delights, but not as doth the law of the Lord thy God." And Augustine adds, "This controversy in my heart was naught but self against self" (VIII, xi).[2] A storm of tears arose in him, and he flung himself down under a fig tree, when he heard the voice as of a boy or girl, he could not tell which, chanting over and over, "Take up and read, take up and read." And Augustine rose and returned to the place where Alypius was sitting and picked up the Book of the Apostles he had left there. His eye fell on the words, "Not in rioting and drunkenness, not in chambering and wantonness, not in strife and envying; but put ye on the Lord Jesus Christ, and make not provision for the flesh, to fulfill the lusts thereof."[3]

It was over. "No further would I read, nor did I need; for instantly, as the sentences ended—by a light, as it were, of security infused into my heart—all the gloom of doubt vanished away." Augustine told Alypius, whose faith was strengthened, and they went in to Monnica, who leaped

[2] Continence was repeating the words of *Colossians* iii, 5.
[3] *Romans,* xiii; *Confessions,* VIII, xii.

for joy. She had triumphed, and she blessed the Lord. "And thou didst turn her grief into a gladness, much more plentiful than she desired, and much dearer and chaster than she used to crave, by having grandchildren of my body" (VIII, xxi).

What had happened? Augustine had tried to secure his mother's love by demonstrating his virility in the manner his father admired and women could not resist. But his mother considered extravagant sexual activity to be a fault. From the first, she had disapproved of his sexuality and demanded that he renounce it as the price of her love. Such a renunciation he refused to make. He feared the loss of his father's and friends' respect: "These appeared to me womanish counsels which I should blush to obey." However, he learned that if he accepted his mother's way of life he could gain entrance into a religious brotherhood and earn the love of the male God who had himself achieved divinity by renouncing his sexuality. Suddenly he became aware that by obeying his mother he could also command the love of his father and of other men as well. The decision to give in to this virtual emasculation was fraught with anguish, and the end came with the auditory hallucination of a sexless voice, whether of a boy or a girl he could not tell, calling on him to read—Augustine knowing very well the sort of admonition he would find. Some two years earlier he had planned to help set up an ideal philosophic community in which he might live a life of continuous pleasure. Now he had attained even more by reuniting himself with his parents and approving himself with the voice he had inherited from his mother, and experiencing something of the unmitigated pleasure he had felt when his mother and father both loved and admired him.

To put the nature of conversion in a general way, we know that the psyche is constantly at work, not only during the waking hours, but even during light sleep, trying always to find the means of gratifying instinctual impulses without violating either the prohibitions of the superego or the facts of reality. When the demands are vigorous and the solution hard to arrive at, the problem-solving activity becomes visibly agitating. As proposed solutions are psychically tested, a succession of unpleasant emotions fills consciousness. And then, when a satisfactory solution is suddenly encountered, its contemplation is accompanied by sudden ecstatic pleasure. The solution may be an insight of inner origin, or a new pattern of social behavior, the acceptance, for example, of religious obligation and humility. The chief obstacle to the solution is the usual demand of religious authority to curtail instinctual pleasure. When the obstacle is overcome, the satisfaction of the superego is often spoken out in an inspiring supervisory voice that is heard as if from without.

While in individual cases, any of a large number of fantasies may be operative, in many it is clear that a specific fantasy of rebirth is being acted out. This fantasy is normally quickened at the transitional moments of change between one condition or epoch of life and another, at puberty and marriage, for instance, and it is accompanied by an overwhelming optimistic pleasure. It is for this reason that those who have been converted often speak of themselves as having been reborn, of having entered into a new life. They sometimes even begin numbering their years from the date of the conversion, much as Western civilization numbers its years from the birth of Christ. The rebirth fantasy fits the phenomenon of conversion well. The antecedent emotional travail is interpreted as the labor of birth. The new insight is spoken of as "seeing the light" or "the new day."

The zeal of the convert to impose his new convictions on others, his aggression bolstered by his sense of righteousness, is so common a result of the conversion that it indicates the operation of a general principle. One may reasonably speculate that it is the inevitable rebound from passivity and submission to activity and aggression, a rebound that makes the conversion more attractive. However, the whole subject requires study. It would be important to know the social, moral, and political conditions that make for conversion, to know whether men or women, and which types of persons, are especially susceptible to conversion, and which converts devote themselves to a private or mild faith and which to the persecution of others. Information can be gathered from the biographies and writings of converts, and more nearly definitive data from the psychoanalysis of converts.

PROPHECY

The prophet asserts some urgent attitude toward life, whether in its moral, social, or political aspect. The emotional intensity of his attitude suggests that its consequences project themselves into the future as an accomplished fact. The intensity, which is also a demand to be heard, tells the sincere prophet, who then tells his hearers, that what he believes, even the very words he speaks in, well out of a more than natural source. He delivers his prophecy while "possessed"; or the "possession" occurs while he is alone and the prophecy is a report of it. The concept of possession arises out of the attempt to explain the overwhelming feeling that a mortal has supernatural sources of inspiration, strength, and wisdom. Essentially, it is the idea that the prophet contains within himself the supernatural being or some part or effective symbol of it. In psychoanalytic terminology, the prophet is said to identify with the divinity by incorporating. The prophet may breathe in the spirit, be inspired—in Hebrew, the same word, *ruach,* is used for both spirit and wind. Or the prophet may consume the sacred substance, as in a ritual meal. Or the spirit may make a sexual entry through some orifice, and a pregnancy fantasy may result. If these unconscious fantasies are kept in mind, the significance of the prophet's figures of speech, which are not merely figurative, becomes clear. Of course, the concept of possession is also applied to the influence of malevolent spirits, the person possessed acquiring supernatural powers for evil. Thus one speaks of a prophet of the devil. Psychologically, the content of a prophecy is explained as produced by the prophet himself, who ascribes it unconsciously to a parent and consciously to a divine being.

Auditory or visual hallucinations often lend the prophet his sense of conviction, for to him they are perceptual proof that what he anticipates will really occur. The core around which the hallucinations form may be sensory phenomena such as flashes of light, or floating shapes, of purely subjective origin. The hallucination is like a dream symbol.

One of the most frequent subjects of prophecy is that of the end of the world. This is the projected sense of foreboding of the prophet. Schizophrenic paranoia is often heralded by fantasies of a cataclysmic death of the world, representing the destruction of the psychic world of the affected man. In the course of such paranoia there may also arise fantasies of the birth of a new world. These represent the attempt to create a world withdrawn from intolerable reality, as if the person, finding that experience had turned colorless, had opened his eyes inwardly to see the serried wish-castles on the intimate landscapes the mind fashions to replace the frightening external vistas. The fantasies are the reinforcements of a retreated psyche, the sentinels of paranoia who guard against the intrusion of the reality that besieges it on all sides. This theme will recur in the pages on religion and psychosis.

Sincere prophecy does not necessarily have neurotic or psychotic impulses. In some communities prophecy is the medium of the politician (the name is not meant invidiously) who is convinced he can foresee the future. To cast his conviction in the form of prophecy is to convince others. As in the case of the Hebrew prophets, the prophetic description may follow the fact and strengthen the allusions to the future, which are made in the same tense and tone. Such prophecy has been more widespread than is usually suspected. There are interesting illustrations of it from among the Gallas, a people of herders, hunters, and warriors, who live in Somaliland and Ethiopia. The prophecies may begin and end with a formula: "Let not the word of Giggo Bacco [the man speaking] go forth from thy head, let it not go forth from thy heart." And their content, for example, is as follows:

> The King of Kaffa will sell the Amhara for a piece of salt; at the price of a *barcu* he will sell the mules: this I prophesy. But in the end, the Amhara will occupy the country of Kaffa. The kingdom of Kaffa will not pass to the son [of the present king]. . . . The emperor will make the slaves and the Galla, the blacksmiths and the Amhara, like brothers, and will have them marry. Such an emperor will come. When this emperor shall reign, the times will become better. . . . He will reign twenty-seven years. . . .[4]

[4] E. Cerulli, *The Folk-Literature of the Galla of Southern Abyssinia*, Cambridge, U.S.A., 1922, p. 182. Quoted in H. M. and N. K. Chadwick, *The Growth of Literature*, Cambridge, England, 1940, vol. iii, pp. 563-64.

Too little is known of the Galla prophets for it to be said with certainty that they would be classed as healthy by a modern psychiatrist. But they do not seem to have shared the demonstrative derangement of the seer who shows symptoms of epilepsy or hysteria, as in Tahiti:

> Tahiti also had its prophetic class, in addition to other *tohungas* who are more or less official priests, and who lay no claim to divine inspiration. Sometimes the priest slept all night near the idol, and received his communication in a dream; at other times the message was divined in the cry of a bird, or in the shrill squeaking articulations of some of the priests. The most interesting and important way of delivering the oracle, however, was when the god "entered the priest, who, inflated. . . . with the divinity, ceased to speak as a voluntary agent, but moved and spoke as entirely under supernatural influence." At such times his dissociated condition seems to have been complete. With shrill cries and foaming mouth he revealed the will of the god, which the attendant priests received and interpreted to the people. Sometimes the possession lasted two or three days. Mama, a chief of the Eimeo in this Group, assured the missionaries that although he sometimes feigned the fits of inspiration, yet at times they came on him unawares and irresistibly.[5]

Among the hysterical phenomena that resemble prophecy are automatic writing, drawing, and painting. The drawings, writings, or paintings, are transformed memories and concealed wish fulfillments that escape the censorship of consciousness, which is kept drowsy, much as they escape it in dreams. The drawer (or prophet) feels himself the tool of an external force—actually of an impulse pro-

[5] H. M. and N. K. Chadwick, *op. cit.*, p. 452. The inner quotation is from W. Ellis, *Polynesian Researches*, London, 1829, vol. ii, p. 234.

jected outward to escape one's own interdiction. The persecutions of the Protestants in France at the end of the seventeenth and the beginning of the eighteenth century set off an epidemic of prophesying among the persecuted, The famous pastor, Marion, testified:

> I declare before God that I do not feel myself in any way solicited or seduced by anyone to utter certain words that the Spirit itself establishes in making use of my organs; and in my ecstasies it is to the Spirit that I abandon the government of my tongue, not occupying my mind except to attend to the words my mouth is reciting. I therefore think that it is a superior power that makes me speak; I do not meditate and I do not know in advance the things that I am going to say; while I speak my mind pays attention to that which my mouth pronounces as if it were a discourse made by someone else, but which usually leaves more or less vivid impressions in my memory.[6]

The prophets by epidemic writhed, threw themselves on their backs on the earth, closed their eyes, and spoke. They saw the open skies, the angels, and Paradise and Hell. The scenes must have resembled the Kentucky Revival that broke out about 1800, in anticipation of the end of the world in 1805. The believers collected in camps.

> [They] "remained on the ground night and day, listening to the most exciting sermons and engaging in a mode of worship which consisted in alternate crying, laughing, singing, and shouting, accompanied with gesticulations of a

[6] From the *Théâtre Sacré des Cévennes,* a collection of statements made in England after the "epidemic" by Protestant refugees who had resisted the king's soldiers. Quoted in G. Dumas, *Le Surnaturel et les dieux d'après les maladies mentales,* Paris, 1946, p. 175.

most extraordinary character. Often there would
be an unusual outcry; some bursting forth into
loud ejaculations of thanksgiving; others exhorting their careless friends to 'turn to the Lord';
some struck with terror, and hastening to escape,
others trembling, weeping, and swooning away,
till every appearance of life was gone, and the
extremity of the body assumed the coldness of a
corpse. At one meeting not less than a thousand
persons fell to the ground, apparently without
sense or motion. It was common to see them shed
tears plentifully about an hour before they fell.
They were then seized with a general tremor, and
sometimes they uttered one or two piercing
shrieks in the moment of falling. This latter
phenomenon was common to both sexes, to all
ages, and to all sorts of characters."

After a time these crazy performances in the
sacred name of religion became so much a matter
of course that they were regularly classified in
categories as the rolls, the jerks, the barks, etc.
"The rolling exercise was effected by doubling
themselves up, then rolling from one side to the
other like a hoop, or in extending the body
horizontally and rolling over and over in the
filth like so many swine. The jerk consisted in
violent spasms and twistings of every part of the
body. Sometimes the head was so twisted round
that the head was turned to the back, and the
countenance so much distorted that not one of
its features was to be recognized. When attacked
by the jerks, they sometimes hopped like frogs,
and the face and limbs underwent the most
hideous contortions. The bark consisted in throwing themselves down on all fours, growling,
showing their teeth, and barking like dogs.
Sometimes a number of people crouching down
in front of the minister continued to bark as he
preached. These last were supposed to be more

especially endowed with gifts of prophecy, dreams, rhapsodies, and visions of angels."[7]

These people were combining hysterical with ritual behavior, the psychic roots of the two being alike, on the whole. The epidemic hysterical ritual got a quick response because each of the Revivalists was serving similar inner needs, and for a short while a social group was sanctioning a relieving hysteria that ordinarily might not be indulged in. The hysteria itself is the mimicry of a psychic war, a mimicry in which there is an attempt to satisfy the superego on the one hand and the forbidden impulse on the other. But in most of us even the mimicry is not allowed to come so boldly to the surface unless society loosens its tight hold on the reins that curb us in.

MYSTICISM

If any single characteristic defines mysticism, it is the feeling of direct experience of a superlative reality, an experience that carries the certainty that nothing is really separate from another, but that everything is one and one alone. But rather than speak of mysticism in general, it may be better to begin with a particular group, and a good group to choose would be the Sufis, Moslem mystics, whose doctrine took shape during the ninth century.

Like most mystics, the Sufis believed that the sole reality is God. They thought that the human soul emanates directly from God, and that human reason is a part of the universal reason. Man's love is given him by God from His infinite store, and from God there proceeds the illumination through which a mystic knows Him who is all there is.

[7] J. Mooney, *Publications of the Bureau of Ethnology, 14* (1892-93), part ii, pp. 942-43. Quoted by R. L. Faris, *Social Disorganization,* New York, 1948, pp. 308-09.

As usual with mystics, the Sufis declared that the mystical experience could not be understood by the intellect alone or conveyed through words. They told the story of the moths who were tormented by their desire to unite themselves with the candle. The moths sent out two of their number, who returned and described the candle as well as they were able to, but they failed to help.

> A third moth rose up, intoxicated with love, to hurl himself violently into the flame of the candle. He threw himself forward and stretched out his antennae towards the flame. As he entered completely into its embrace, his members became red like the flame itself. When the wise moth saw from afar that the candle had identified the moth with itself, and had given to it its own light, he said: "This moth has accomplished his desire; but he alone comprehends that to which he has attained. None other knows it, and that is all."[8]

The experience is one of intense joy. The Sufi poet sees Time and Space crouching at his feet. He feels the universal Center within himself, its wonder circumscribed about him. But the joy is preceded by doubt and pain, and intensified, it may be, by a masochistic coloration:

> A lover sets fire to the whole harvest: he puts the knife to his own throat, and pierces his own body. Torment and affliction are what pertain to love: Love expects difficult things.[9]

The mystical experience is thus the most intense form of love. In the words of al-Ghazali, the greatest of the Sufi philosophers, the search is initiated by a feeling of lack of love:

[8] Margaret Smith, *The Persian Mystics: Attar*, London, 1932, p. 52.
[9] *Ibid.*, p. 48.

> Contrition results from the realisation that sin intervenes between the sinner and the Beloved; it is the grief of the heart when it becomes aware of the absence of the Beloved.[10]

Plotinus, the greatest mystical philosopher who entered into the European tradition directly, also said that the experience is a love for lofty beauties above the beauties of visible things:

> In the sense-bound life we are no longer granted to know them, but the soul, taking no help from the organs, sees and proclaims them. To the vision of these we must mount, leaving sense in its own low place. . . . Such vision is for those only who see with the Soul's sight—and at the vision, they will rejoice, and awe will fall upon them. . . . This is the spirit that Beauty must ever induce, wonderment and a delicious trouble, longing and love and a trembling that is all delight.[11]

Whether or not such experiences are wholly derived from childhood, and whether or not they indicate the truth, they are at least partial returns to and reminiscences of the infantile stage of life. At first all of our perceptions are referred to our own bodies, from which the environment that touches on us is not clearly distinguished. The needs for elimination and food are the chief disturbances. We are hungry and awake and cry, and then we suck at a breast or bottle, swallow the milk, and fall asleep peacefully again. In the sense that the breast is perceived by the baby as part of itself, so is the mother. Mother love and milk are both assimilated into ourselves together, and, as has been said, a real or fancied loss of love is often compensated by an abnormal appetite for food. And any psychic trouble

[10] Margaret Smith, *Al-Ghazali the Mystic,* London, 1944, p. 153.
[11] *Enneads of Plotinus,* I.6.4, translated by S. McKenna, vol. i, p. 82.

in later life is likely to drive us back to our primitive pleasures, to the stage in which the baby has something akin to a sense of omnipotence, and feels an irradiating pleasure from which all the pleasures of later life, including the erotic, will separate out.

It would therefore not be surprising to discover that mystics are so troubled by the world of their maturity that they tend to retreat toward the omnipotence of infancy and its undifferentiated pleasure. Plotinus would tell his disciples

> how, at the age of eight, when he was already going to school, he still clung about his nurse and loved to bare her breasts and take suck: one day he was told he was a "perverted imp," and so was shamed out of the trick.[12]

The tendency to retreat and to demand the love and security granted an infant had already been established, and his later longing to join God in a union of love was a reappearance on a new level of the old desire.

The feeling of one's own omnipotence is succeeded by that of one's parents' omnipotence. The parents enter our conscience, and their approval becomes our self-approval. When we join a cause that fills our whole psychic horizon (when, for instance, we revel in patriotism) we are again identifying ourselves with something so powerful that it unconsciously recalls our parent-gods and arouses an exaltation that harks back to our pleasure in their love. In one of the legends about Meister Eckhart, the German mystic (1260-1328), a boy appears before him and Eckhart asks where he comes from. The answer is, "I come from God." Eckhart asks where he left God, and the answer

[12] From Porphyry's life of Plotinus. *Enneads of Plotinus,* trans. Mc-Kenna, vol. 1, p. 3.

is, "In virtuous hearts." And then he asks where he is going, and the boy says, "To God."[13] The Sufi saint Dhu 'l-Nun recalled that he once saw an old woman carrying a staff and wearing a woolen tunic coming toward him. He asked her where she came from, and she answered, "From God." Then he asked her where she was going. "To God," she said.[14] So far as the unconscious mind goes, these identical answers may be interpreted to mean that the travelers wish to return to the infant's unmitigated pleasure and to their omnipotent parents with whom they have identified themselves and their conscience in particular. God, the father, as the boy said to Eckhart, dwells in virtuous, obedient hearts.

The mystic's conviction of the unity of the world is usually based on his feeling that the visible world is unreal, an unstable dream, a mere reflection on the face of the water, which their conscious fantasies as the only reality. As the mystic retreats, or, as he would put it, as he goes forward, the usual world goes grey. The retreat and the self-absorption are very well conveyed in a humorous parable used by the Taoists, Chinese mystics:

> There was a man in Sung by the name of Huatse, who developed in his middle age a peculiar malady of forgetting everything. He would take a thing in the morning and forget about it at night, and receive a thing at night and forget about it in the morning. While in the streets he forgot to walk, and while standing in the house, he forgot to sit down. He could not remember the past in the present, and could not remember the present in the future. And the whole family were

[13] R. B. Blakney, *Meister Eckhart*, New York, 1941, p. 251.
[14] R. A. Nicholson, *The Kashf al-Mahjub, The Oldest Persian Treatise on Sufiism*, London, 1936 (2nd ed.), p. 89.

greatly annoyed by it. They consulted the sooth-
sayer and they could not divine it, and they consulted the witch and prayers would not cure it,
and they consulted the physician and the physician
was helpless. But there was a Confucian scholar in
the country of Lu who said that he could cure
him. So the family of Huatse offered him half of
their property if he should cure him of this
strange malady. And the Confucian scholar said:

"His malady is not something which can be
cured by soothsaying or prayer or medicine. I
shall try to cure his mind and change the objects
of his thought, and maybe he'll be cured."

So he exposed Huatse to cold and Huatse asked
for clothing, exposed Huatse to hunger, and
Huatse asked for food, and shut Huatse up in a
dark room, and Huatse asked for light. So he kept
him in a room all by himself for seven days and
cared not what he was doing all this time. And
the illness of years was cured in a day.

When Huatse was cured and learned about it,
he was furious. He scolded his wife and punished
his children and drove away the Confucian scholar
from his house with a spear. The people of the
country asked Huatse why he did so, and Huatse
replied:

"When I was submerged in the sea of forgetfulness, I did not know whether the heaven and
earth existed or not. Now they have waked me up,
and all the successes and disappointments and
joys and sorrows and loves and hatreds of the past
decades have come back to disturb my breast.
I am afraid that in the future, the successes and
disappointments and joys and sorrows and loves
and hatreds will continue to oppress my mind as
they are oppressing me now. Can I ever recover
even a moment of forgetfulness?"[15]

[15] From the book of Liehtse. In Lin Yutang, *The Wisdom of India and
China,* New York, 1942, pp. 1057-58.

The mystic makes a radical attempt to shut external stimuli out of his life. He may in his effort to enter deeply into himself evolve a psychic technique and a theory of stages of withdrawal (or approach). He may go so far as to think that consciousness can be erased and some super-consciousness entered, though even the latter name may seem to him to suggest that which he wants to escape. A traditional recital of the death of Buddha indicates the stepwise elaboration of the process:

> The Lord attained the first trance. Arising from the first trance he attained the second. Arising from the second he attained the third. Arising from the third he attained the fourth. Arising from the fourth he attained the stage of the infinity of space. Arising from the stage of the infinity of space he attained the stage of the infinity of consciousness. Arising from the stage of the infinity of consciousness he attained the stage of nothingness. Arising from the stage of nothingness he attained the stage of neither perception nor non-perception.
>
> Arising from the stage of neither perception nor non-perception he attained the stage of nothingness. Arising from the stage of nothingness he attained the stage of the infinity of consciousness. Arising from the stage of the infinity of consciousness he attained the stage of the infinity of space. Arising from the stage of the infinity of space he attained the fourth trance. Arising from the fourth trance he attained the third. Arising from the third he attained the second. Arising from the second he attained the first.
>
> Arising from the first trance he attained the second. Arising from the second he attained the third. Arising from the third he attained the

fourth. Arising from the fourth the Lord straight-
way attained Nirvana.[16]

The state that is attained by a mystic is a state of euphoria
or ecstasy in which the outer world seems to vanish and
the self to stretch out, lose its boundaries, and engulf everything. This is simultaneously a projection of the self into
the whole environment and an introjection of the whole
environment into the self. It is a return to what some
psychoanalysts call the "oceanic reunion," the world of
the fed, satisfied baby on the delicious edge of sleep. All
one's pleasure impulses are withdrawn from external
objects and located inside oneself. And the variegated
responses of the mind are narrowed and merged until
they approximate the semiconscious, slumbrous, undifferentiated pleasure of the baby immersed in the uniform
ocean of his feeling. It is a state of both omnipotence and
dependence, and often the mystic feels his absorption to
be a happy helplessness in which a force that is greater than
himself but includes himself handles him as a parent
handles the little child.

Abu Hafs, a Sufi, was a blacksmith. One day, after his
return from a trip he took for the purpose of studying,

. . . . he was sitting in his shop listening to a blind
man who was reciting the Koran in the bazaar.
He became so absorbed in listening that he put
his hand into the fire and, without using the
pincers, drew out a piece of molten iron from the
furnace. On seeing this the apprentice fainted.
When Abu Hafs came to himself he left his shop
and no longer earned his livelihood. It is related
that he said: "I left work and returned to it; then
work left me and I never returned to it again."

[16] E. J. Thomas, *Early Buddhist Scriptures*, London, 1935, p. 52.

And the commentator explains that whatever a man does through his own efforts is comparatively worthless. It is God's choice that is decisive.

> Man cannot properly take or leave anything; it is God who in His providence gives and takes away, and Man only takes what God has given or leaves what God has taken away. Though a disciple should strive a thousand years to win the favour of God, it would be worth less than if God received him into favour for a single moment, since everlasting happiness is involved in the favour of past eternity, and Man has no means of escape except by the unalloyed bounty of God.[17]

Whether the commentator is right or wrong, the favor of God wears the aspect of the mother's smile, and the mystic gives himself up to God like the baby who does little but lie and cry and submit himself to his good parents. The commentator even feels, unconsciously, that a parent's love is worth more when spontaneous than when elicited by the efforts of the baby. (This paragraph is not meant to imply that mystics may not be active in worldly affairs. It describes the mystical experience alone.)

If the mystic feels that he is being handled by a greater power than himself but which is himself, he regards himself as a spectator would regard a stranger. That he feels united with God cuts him off from the "unreal" part of himself. This is the feeling expressed by a modern Hindu philosopher in telling of his past life:

> I travelled from place to place, depending mainly on alms cooked or uncooked, whatever chance would bring to me. I always held in my mind the thought that the phenomenal world was transitory and unreal; that I was a spectator like

[17] R. A. Nicholson, *op. cit.*, pp. 124-25.

the unchangeable Atman of Vedanta which always remains a witness of the games which people were playing in the world. In this manner I endured all sorts of privation and hardship, practised austerities of all kinds, walked up to the sources of the Jamuna and the Ganges, where I stayed for three months in the caves of the Himalayas at the altitude of nearly 14,000 feet above the sea level, spending most of my time in the contemplation of the Absolute, I realised that the phenomenal world was like a dream.[18]

To such a mystic the body is a husk that must be cast off. Like many schizophrenics, he is estranged from his person. He has the constant feeling of "depersonalization" that normal men have only from time to time. That is, his feeling of guilt at his desires succeeds in masking the desires and even the bodily experiences that constitute the core of the sense of self. He recognizes impulses, but they are muted and distant. The mystic has split himself in two. The part that his conscience approves and his mystical experience validates he calls "real."

A further reaction of mystics seems at first to be the opposite of the conviction of the worthlessness of the outer world. As the French writer, Amiel, put the feeling:

One day, in youth, at sunrise, sitting in the ruins of the castle of Faucigny; and again in the mountains, under the noonday sun, above Lavey, lying at the foot of a tree and visited by three butterflies; once more at night upon the shingly shore of the Northern Ocean, my back upon the sand and my vision ranging through the milky way;— such grand and spacious, immortal, cosmogonic reveries, when one reaches to the stars, when one

[18] Swami Abhedananda, in *Contemporary Indian Philosophy*, edited by S. Radhakrishnan and J. H. Muirhead, New York, 1936, p. 50.

owns the infinite! Minutes divine, ecstatic hours; in which our thought flies from world to world, pierces the great enigma, breathes with a respiration broad, tranquil, and deep as the respiration of the ocean, serene and limitless as the blue firmament; . . . instants of irresistible intuition in which one feels one's self great as the universe, and calm as a god. . . . What hours, what memories! The vestiges they leave behind are enough to fill us with belief and enthusiasm, as if they were visits of the Holy Ghost.[19]

The world feels infinitely valuable. It is not grey and dull, but bright and utterly marvelous. We try to assimilate all the universe because it glows in the light of the happiness we shed on it. Instead of retreating inward we expand outward into the cosmogonic, ecstatic, serene, and breathing ocean, the adult counterpart of the child's cosmogonic ocean. But whether we retreat inward or expand outward, it is ourselves we have found and our own breathing to which the world keeps time.

[19] Amiel, *Journal Intime*, quoted by William James in *The Varieties of Religious Experience*, Modern Library ed., p. 386.

CHAPTER 8

Disintegration

PSYCHIC DISINTEGRATION

IT IS not hard to theorize on the effect of religiousness on mental health. Religion is specifically directed against guilt and depression, and unless it takes a pathological turn, one would expect the devout to suffer less from the psychic diseases that are marked by guilt and depression. On the other hand, religion characteristically reduces the emphasis on strict theoretical and empirical validation. It tends to rest on faith, to obliterate the differences between the data of direct perception and the other contents of the mind (fantasies, desires, aversions), and to condemn the demands for factual proof. One might therefore suppose religion to reinforce schizophrenic tendencies.

But such theories are more easily stated than proved. There is not enough large-scale evidence for any secure conclusion on the effect of religion on psychic disease. We do know that there are deeply religious people who have become schizophrenic, and others who have been depressed. Neurosis among the religious often expresses itself in the form of obsessive doubts, or of an obsessive impulse to violate a religious law. A clergyman might, for instance, feel an overpowering desire to blaspheme during the service he was conducting.

Individual observations, however, whether those of Jung, who found religion to be a defense against neurosis, or of anyone else, must always remain insufficient. They can never have the evidential force of adequate statistics. Unfortunately, adequate statistics on such problems are lacking and are tremendously hard to gather. If it is found that in a given canton in Switzerland fewer Catholics visit psychiatrists, several possible grounds of explanation are immediately evident. Perhaps a Catholic has more scruples against consulting a psychiatrist. Perhaps Catholics in this canton have a social or economic position that subjects them to less strain. It is not simply that they may be wealthier, a difference in status that is easy to make out. Under certain circumstances poverty may maintain the psyche with greater effectiveness than wealth—Negroes are said to have a low suicide rate—and we have more than once described the sort of person who is kept mentally healthy by misfortune. It is also possible that the religious group we are considering has a traditional family organization or a traditional way of rearing children that has no necessary connection with its dogmas, but which is primarily responsible for its differential status with respect to mental health.

Statistics are available that might seem to offer good evidence, but they do not. The statistics are those on mental hospital admissions, criminality, suicide, and divorce. For statistics on mental hospital admissions to be significant in this case, the different religious groups would have to be equated for income, occupation, region, locality (city, town, village, farm), nonreligious modes of behavior, availability of mental hospitals, degree of reliance on doctors and social agencies, and the like. It is also well known that the rough classifications under which mental patients are categorized in hospital records conceal as much as they reveal.

The same sorts of difficulties surround the judgment of statistics on crime. In the first place, and this applies to all statistical judgments on religion, the figures do not discriminate between a person who joins a church to make friends and business contacts and a person who has strong religious convictions. In the second place, and this consideration also applies to all statistical judgments on religion, age and sex complicate numerical comparisons. The proportion of Roman Catholic children in the United States is relatively high, while that of the Baptists is relatively low. As a result, the proportion of Catholic juvenile delinquents may be misleadingly high, and the proportion of Baptist juvenile delinquents misleadingly low. The sex ratios of the different religious groups also vary. The Baptists and Methodists have had a comparatively large proportion of women, and since most imprisoned criminals are men, the apparent crime rate of these religious groups is lower than it might otherwise be. In addition, many of the Baptists and Methodists are Negroes, and many Catholics and Jews are immigrants or the sons of recent immigrants; and Catholics, Jews, and Negroes, have special adjustments to make in the face of prejudice.

There are other complications too. Shortly before the parole law went into effect in Illinois in 1895, the proportion of inmates registering themselves as church members shot up from 37 per cent to 81 per cent and then went still higher. The explanation given was this:

> The criminal world now knew that not only a good record in prison could help a prisoner regain his liberty, but also outside influences and agencies, including politicians, charity workers

and others, and not least church organizations, who might interest themselves on the prisoner's behalf before the board of parole. . . . Hence the very pardonable effort of incoming prisoners to line up as many friends as possible, especially among charity and church workers; in particular their effort to get the good will of the chaplain, the effort to appear as religious as possible.[1]

In addition, the criminal is differently defined by law in different places, crime is a legal rather than a psychological classification, and one type of criminal may be quite unlike another.

It is needless to go into rates of suicide and divorce, because the problem with respect to them remains the same: crude statistics are highly misleading, simple one-to-one relationships between such inclusive, vague categories as "religion" and "crime," or "religion" and "mental illness" cannot be, or at least have not been found, and the work of refining the statistics sufficiently must be slow and painstaking. Even when such a quasi-religious body as Alcoholics Anonymous appears to give results that are unambiguous, interpretation is not easy. In addition to faith, Alcoholics Anonymous provides each member with a companion, whom he calls when he gets the urge to drink, and this is the use of a psychotherapeutic technique not strictly religious.

For all we have said about statistics, there is a known relationship between religion and some forms of psychosis. The relationship between religion and paranoia is perhaps the most interesting. Paranoid persons are simultaneously most sensitive to the opinions of others and subjective,

[1] Leo Kalmer, *Crime and Religion*, Chicago, Franciscan Herald Press, 1936, pp. 24-25. Quoted in Hans von Hentig, *The Criminal and His Victim*, New Haven, 1948, pp. 334-35.

self-assertive, and unyielding, in their own. They tend to brood and isolate themselves in a fantasy world, which satisfies the impulses the sterner objective world has denied them. When these tendencies grow so dominating that they create a pronounced break with reality they constitute the psychosis of paranoia.

In the sense that paranoiacs reconstruct reality in accord with their own inner needs, they have returned to the childhood level in which there is yet no sharp division between the self and the nonself, and in which impulse may seem all-powerful, able to mold everything in its own shape. The paranoiac, unable to adapt himself to reality, adapts reality to himself; and the less others love him, the more he honors and cherishes his own person. He is Napoleon, he believes, or Alexander the Great, or even God. He has grasped the hidden truth, and with it he will save the world and rise to omnipotence. But not all is necessarily pleasant, because the anxieties of the paranoiac take the shapes of projected, vengeful figures. The paranoiac is usually a person with unconscious homosexual drives who defends himself against his desire by imagining that he hates the object of his love. This projected condemnation by the superego persecutes him, so to speak, and therefore the paranoiac may have delusions of persecution.

William Blake exemplifies the man whose paranoiac delusions enter into the substance of art. His world within, as Blake said, was more important than the external. He would call wildly, "I am Socrates," or "I am the prophet Isaiah." His visions of great historical figures were so clear that he would draw their portraits, looking up from time to time as if the person were sitting beside him. A visitor heard Blake say, "The Spirits told me." This led the visitor to ask:

"Socrates used pretty much the same language
—He spoke of his Genius. Now what affinity or re-
semblance do you suppose was there between the
Genius which inspired Socrates and your *Spirits*?"
He smiled, and for once it seemed to me as if
he had a feeling of vanity gratified—The same as
in our countenances—He paused and said "I was
Socrates"—and then as if he had gone too far in
that—"Or a sort of brother. I must have had con-
versations with him. So I had with Jesus Christ.
I have an obscure recollection of having been with
both of them."[2]

On one occasion Blake "saw" and drew the *Ghost of a
Flea,* a staring humanoid head, suggestive of a skull, its
open mouth displaying a pointed tongue and vindictive
teeth.

During the time occupied in completing the
drawing, the Flea told him that all fleas were
inhabited by the souls of such men as were by
nature blood-thirsty to excess, and were therefore providentially confined to the size and form
of insects; otherwise, were he himself, for instance,
the size of a horse, he would depopulate a great
portion of the country.[3]

We may conjecture that these vindictive fleas represent
Blake's own fantasies of a homosexual aggressor, and their
small size represents Blake's unconscious attempt to overcome them.[4]

Paranoids often display a tendency to make systematic,
pseudo-philosophic classifications of "truths" and symbols.

[2] Alexander Gilchrist, *Life of William Blake,* Everyman's Library, p. 333.
[3] Gilchrist, *op. cit.,* p. 266.
[4] The reconstruction of the unconscious fantasies of an individual from
the appearance of a few symbols in his works is most hazardous. Not only
is the possibility of gross error great, but almost all symbols have multiple
referents in any given individual.

Suddenly they appear to themselves to see through appearances to reality. Their drawings are often symmetrical, symbolic, and hieratic, and represent, like their speech, anxieties and wish fulfillments. They turn easily to religious language, in part, maybe, because their deep early experiences revolve about their parents and the conflict between impulse and superego, which are much the same experiences that religion embodies. Besides, religion is identified with the kind of powerful emotions that may seize the paranoiac. He may make up an elaborate vocabulary to name the various beings he sees.

One paranoiac believed in invisible spirits of the air who, from above the houses, surveyed the movement of pedestrians on the sidewalks. These spirits he called *Tratones*. The *Trémillets*, he said, were invisible spirits that showed you the acts and gestures of dead persons. The *Gleaners* and *Profiters* were invisible spirits that kept coming to eat some of the (mythical) infants of Mrs. Dufoy, and that lived in the trees of Saint-Anne. A *Plurimie* was to him a group of persons living in the same century; a *Pluriple,* a synthetic person made up of several; *Planispherians* were invisible spirits that governed the world; and *Sphéiques* were persons having beauty of the Greek type. These personages and more the paranoiac employed in his own mythology.[5]

Blake's "prophetic books" evolve a paranoid mythology, sometimes with genuine esthetic power. He believed *Jerusalem* to have been dictated to him without his premeditation and even against his will (i.e., he had some fear of revealing his impulses, even in symbolic form, but did so because he was possessed). The poetry shows wish ful-

[5] Georges Dumas, *Le Surnaturel et les dieux d'apres les maladies mentales,* Paris, 1946, p. 303.

fillment, the desire to return to undifferentiated infantile well-being, the desire to surrender passively to his father, and, simultaneously, to defend himself. All these can be found in the following lines, which one might imagine to be an amalgam of the Christian faith with an unknown pagan religion:

> Trembling I sit day and night, my friends are
> astonish'd at me,
> Yet they forgive my wanderings. I rest not from
> my great task!
> To open the Eternal Worlds, to open the im-
> mortal Eyes
> Of Man inwards into the Worlds of Thought, into
> Eternity
> Ever expanding in the Bosom of God, the Human
> Imagination.
> O Saviour pour upon me thy Spirit of meekness
> & love!
> Annihilate the Selfhood in me: be thou all my
> life!
> Guide thou my hand, which trembles exceedingly
> upon the rock of ages,
> While I write of the buildings of Golgonooza, &
> of the terrors of Entuthon,
> Of Hand & Hyle & Coban, of Kwantok, Peachey,
> Brereton, Slayd & Hutton,
> Of terrible sons & daughters of Albion, and
> their Generations.

> Scofield, Knox, Kotope and Bowen revolve most
> mightily upon
> The Furnace of Los; before the eastern gate
> bending their fury
> They war to destroy the Furnaces, to desolate
> Golgonooza,
> And to devour the Sleeping Humanity of Albion
> in rage & hunger.

Paranoiacs have played their role in the history of religion. Characteristically, some of them are unable to gain the friendship of other men on equal terms, and can maintain a relationship with them only as leaders demanding disciples, disciples who, of course, fulfill the leader's wish to be loved, and whose acquiescence assures the leader that his delusions represent reality. An investigation made by a medical missionary intimates rather starkly what may have been true more often than is ordinarily suspected:

> Dr. Pennell, who is well known for his fine work as a medical missionary on the Afghan frontier [and who had studied mental disease], was anxious to learn more of the life of Sadhus [holy men] and decided that the best way was to adopt their dress and habits and travel among them. Accordingly he put on the ochre-coloured robe and begged his way to Rishikesh, a colony of Sadhus near Hardwar. There he was admitted without question as a Christian ascetic and moved freely among the Hindus—a remarkable example of Hindu toleration. He found that some Sadhus were imbeciles, others suffered from delusional insanity, others from mania, acute in some cases, more or less chronic in others, or passing into a drivelling dementia. One man asserted that he was a cow in human form and must therefore eat nothing but grass and roots; another ran about stark naked barking like a dog; a third picked up and chewed bits of filth and ordure. On the other hand, as Dr. Pennell was careful to point out, many were earnest seekers after a higher spiritual life and unostentatiously devout, one of them being a former Prime Minister of an Indian State. These, however, were a minority, "gems amongst the rubble," found "side by side with the basest

charlatans and the most immoral caricatures of their own ideals."[6]

The chief difficulty results from the fact that some paranoiacs appear normal in every respect, except for their delusions, which they may successfully conceal for a long time. It is usual to distinguish between paranoid schizophrenics and "true" paranoids, whose general conduct is normal, whose intelligence may be good, and whose personality remains, on the whole, well organized—even though complete recovery is rare. Two cases of apparently true paranoia that the authors have seen may serve to illustrate something of its nature.

The first is that of a man of quite low intelligence and ability, who claimed he was the founder of a new Judaism. He knew only the Hebrew alphabet, out of which he made nonsense syllables he endowed with a mystical meaning. He also drew symbolic diagrams. Otherwise he seemed to be normal.

The second case is that of a highly intelligent Texan aviation mechanic. His belief that he had a supernatural revelation led him to found a new Christian church, for which he had in the course of time gained ten members. During the Second World War he refused to comply with Selective Service regulations, although he was assured he would be deferred because of physical disability. He was surely sincere, and surely an otherwise efficient, intelligent man.

When someone's personality is openly disintegrating, he is not likely to delude many followers. But when he looks strong, sane, resourceful, and convinced of the truth of his

[6] L. S. S. O'Malley, *Popular Hinduism,* New York and Cambridge, England, 1935, p. 213. The inner quotation is from T. L. Pennell, *Among the Wild Tribes of the Afghan Frontier,* 1909.

visions, the matter is otherwise. As in the case of the mystics, with whom the paranoid may often be classed, there is a contest of rival "realities," his reality against the conventional one. The issue then becomes one of epistemology or metaphysics, with which we cannot deal here. Perhaps, at the minimum, the same test may be made of a vision as Bergson thought wise for an intuition. Paranoids, indeed, are always "intuiting" what the rest of us are not able to. Bergson, who stressed the value of intuitions, nevertheless wanted to distinguish between the true and the delusive or apparent. He urged a pragmatic test. An intuition that proves itself fruitful, the consequences of which can be intellectually developed and applied to useful ends, is to be considered true. On the other hand, the feeling of revelation experienced by a man who has not investigated a problem with all the available human resources, or that proves itself fruitless in application and intellectually sterile, is to be considered false.

Since reality has been conceived in different ways by different cultures, the defining traits of paranoia must be culturally conditioned, especially because the more objective test of personality disintegration cannot be easily applied in many instances. Shamans and medicine men have typically sought after visions, and we ourselves still honor ancient visionaries. The selfsame conditions that would cause us to explain away an experience as hallucinatory, would cause an Eskimo to accept it as revelatory:

> My novitiate took place in the middle of the coldest winter and I, who never got anything to warm me must not move, was very cold, and it was so tiring having to sit without daring to lie down, that sometimes it was as if I died a little. Only towards the end of the thirty days did a helping spirit come to me, a lovely and beautiful helping

spirit, whom I had never thought of. It was a white woman. She came to me whilst I had collapsed, exhausted, and was sleeping. But still I saw her lifelike hovering over me, and from that day I could not close my eyes or dream without seeing her. . . . Later, when I had quite become myself again, I understood that I had become the shaman of my village, and it did happen that my neighbors or people from a long distance away called to me to heal a sick person or to "inspect a course" if they were going to travel. When this happened, the people of my village were called together and I told them what I had been asked to do. Then I left the tent or snow house and went out into solitude, away from the dwellings of man. But those who remained behind had to sing continuously, just to keep themselves happy and lively.

These days of "seeking for knowledge" are very tiring, for one must walk all the time, no matter what the weather is like, and only rest in short snatches. I am usually quite done up, tired, not only in body but also in head, when I have found what I sought.[7]

A culture such as the Eskimo favors a paranoid personality, whereas ours, in most cases, does not. Certainly we are not inclined to believe in the white woman of the vision, though we have accepted other beliefs with the same sort of warrant. But even those of us who have adopted the most matter-of-fact criteria should be able to feel sympathy for the shaman who said:

True wisdom is only to be found far away from the people, out in great solitude, and it is not to

[7] K. Rasmussen, *Intellectual Culture of the Caribou Eskimo,* Report of the Fifth Thule Expedition, 1921-1924, vol. vii, no. 2. In Paul Radin, *Primitive Religion,* New York, 1937, pp. 112, 113.

be found in play but only through suffering. Solitude and suffering open the human mind, and therefore a shaman must seek his wisdom there.[8]

The shaman was defining the conditions under which he could stimulate the projection of the symbols of his psychic life, symbols which then took on the double representation of inner and outer life, the latter constituted by the tensions between the Caribou Eskimos and their environment. Thus the vision represents both the microcosm and the macrocosm, and arising out of the psyche is taken to be the source of power and the seat of the real.

SOCIAL DISINTEGRATION

Since religion is concerned with the government of the impulses, it also expresses resentments and directs aggressiveness. The most peaceable preachers are likely to use an aggressive, militaristic vocabulary. The Epistles of Saint Paul include sentences such as:

> Thou therefore endure hardness, as a good soldier of Jesus Christ. No man that warreth entangleth himself with the affairs of this life; that he may please him who hath chosen him to be a soldier. . . . I have fought a good fight, I have finished my course, I have kept the faith. . . . Paul, a prisoner of Jesus Christ, and Timothy our brother, unto Philemon our dearly beloved, and fellowlabourer, And to our beloved Apphia, and Archippus our fellowsoldier. . . . For the word of God is quick, and powerful, and sharper than any twoedged sword, piercing even to the dividing asunder of soul and spirit, and of the joints and marrow. . . .

[8] Rasmussen, *op. cit.*, p. 55 (Radin, p. 106).

Many Christian classics are alive with warlike words. The very name, *pagan,* assigned to non-Christians was the Latin for *civilian,* and was taken to mean someone not enrolled among the Soldiers of Christ. The Latin *sacramentum* was applied especially to military oaths and oaths of allegiance. The Salvation Army, paradoxically pacific, was originally called the East London Mission. But as it became an army, the annual conference became a council of war; the leaders, a military hierarchy; the watchword, "Blood and Fire." A letter written by the founder of the Salvation Army when he was twenty is a call to battle:

> Grasp still firmer the standard! Unfold still wider the battle flag! Press still closer on the ranks of the enemy, and mark your pathway still more distinctly with glorious trophies of Emmanuel's grace, and with enduring monuments of Jesus' power! The trumpet has given the signal for the conflict! Your general assures you of success, and a glorious reward, your crown, is already held out. Then why delay? Why doubt? Onward! Onward! Be that your motto—be that your battle cry—be that your war note—be that your consolation—be that your plea when asking mercy of God—your end when offering it to man—your hope when encircled by darkness—your triumph and your victory when attacked and overcome by death! Christ for me! Tell it to men who are living and dying in sin! Tell it to Jesus that you have chosen Him to be your Saviour and your God. Tell it to devils, and bid them cease to harass, since you are determined to die for the truth![9]

A metaphorically military assault on evil is able to become a literal one. Some religions, like the Moham-

[9] F. de L. Booth-Tucker, *The Life of Catherine Booth,* London, 1892, vol. i, p. 53. Cited in Pierre Bovet, *The Fighting Instinct,* London, 1923, p. 123.

medan, have an explicit physical militarism. In theory Islam may make temporary truces with the non-Islamic world, but the Mohammedans stand under an unceasing obligation to conquer and try to convert those who have not awakened to the Mohammedan truth. The *hadith,* the sacred tradition supposed to descend from Mohammed, says:

> Frontier duty for one day in the way of God is better than the world and all that therein is. . . . Make raids in the way of God! He that contends in the way of God but the time between two milkings of a camel, paradise is his due. . . . He who equips a warrior in the way of God has fought himself; and he who is left behind to take care of a warrior's family has fought himself.[10]

The rewards of a martyr, one who fell in holy warfare, were remission of his sins at the fall of the first drop of blood, a seat in paradise, safety from hell, a crown of dignity with jewels each worth more than the world with all its contents, seventy dark-eyed virgins, and the power to intercede successfully for seventy relatives. To the Moslem, the sword gave entrance to heaven and hell.

While the Moslems set on others with religious fervor, the tables were at times reversed. The Crusaders came at them with religious (and other) enthusiasms. The Sikhs of India, a group that originated in an attempt to reconcile Hinduism with Islam, were at first instructed to "take up arms that will harm no one; let your coat of mail be understanding; convert your enemies into friends; fight with valor, but with no weapon but the word of God." But the

---

[10] Alfred Guillaume, *The Traditions of Islam,* Oxford University Press, 1924, pp. 111-12.

Sikhs fell afoul of the Moslem administration, which tried to suppress them. The tenth leader of the Sikhs had a new psalm to sing:

> I bow to the scimitar and the two-edged sword, to
>   the falchion and also the dagger,
> I bow to the arrow, to the musket and the mace, to
>   lance, shaft, cannon, rapier, and sword.

A Moslem historian describes the warfare between the Sikhs, led by Banda, and the Moslems, in about 1810, in these words:

> Banda set about plundering, having gathered about him pony riders and motley footmen, eighteen or nineteen thousand men in all, with arms. These accursed wretches carried on a cruel and predatory warfare, shouting "True King" and "Victory to the Doctrine." Many Musalmans found martyrdom and many infidels went to the sink of perdition. At the siege of Sirhind the evil dogs fell to murdering the men, making prisoners of the children and the women of the high and low, carrying on atrocities for many days with such violence that they tore open the wombs of pregnant women, dashing every living child upon the ground, set fire to the houses, involving all in common ruin. Wherever they found a mosque or a tomb of a respected Musalman, they demolished the building, dug up the body, and made it not sin to scatter the bones of the dead. When they had done with the pillage of Sirhind, they went off to Delhi, where the Musalmans made against the villainous foe a manly resistance and sent many of the enemy to hell. . . . These infidels had set up a new rule, and had forbidden the shaving of the hair of the head and the beard. Many ill-

disposed, low-caste Hindus had joined themselves to them, and, placing their lives at the disposal of these evil-minded people, found their own advantage in professing belief and obedience, and they were very active in persecuting and killing other castes of Hindus.[11]

Needless to say, a Sikh account of the warfare would be different; but warfare it was, and warfare intimately allied with religion. Religion can become socially disruptive. The aggressiveness that each of us is forced to contain within himself does not evaporate. It may be turned inward as self-excoriation for sins, real or imaginary. It may be turned outward as prejudice against other groups. Or it may be simultaneously turned both inward and outward in war, in which one sacrifices comfort and sometimes life in order to overcome an enemy. The soldier, as a soldier, has two enemies, the opposing army and his impulse to live; and three allies, the army to which he belongs, and his impulses to kill and to die as his conscience directs. Like every other social institution, religion often thwarts the good it seems designed to accomplish. It organizes men and keeps them at peace, and yet at times it undoes its work and sets them at war against one another.

[11] John C. Archer, *The Sikhs*, Princeton University Press, 1946, pp. 170, 203, 212, 213.

CHAPTER 9

Psychiatry and the Truth of Religion

THERE is a time for explanation and a time for reckoning, and the time for reckoning is now at hand. It is not primarily philosophic controversies we are dealing with. To tell the truth, which the history of philosophy demonstrates with admirable candor and industrious hope, there is nothing by way of assured conclusions that philosophy can lend to the judgment. Intelligent men come no closer to agreement after studying the endlessly elaborated arguments than before. We do not mean to imply that the force of the reasoning on both sides is exactly equal, or that we ourselves are neutral in the debate; but competent, learned thinkers have arrived at no consensus of opinion. Wherever the truth about religion may be, it does not proclaim itself from the hilltops.

Refinements aside, the argument that the causes and effects that constitute nature must have had a first, uncaused cause, receives the answer that experience never reveals any absolute beginnings or gives any warrant for believing in them. If, when we consider time, space, electrons, and other elementals, we think it legitimate to ask, "And what made these?" it is equally legitimate to ask the child's question, "And what made God?" If, on the other hand, we refuse to ask the second question, we might as well refuse to ask the first. Nor is a universe with no beginning any more difficult to conceive than one that began or was created from nothing.

The belief in a first cause thought of as prior in its reality is supported by a plentiful species of arguments, cousins to the Platonic opinion that material things are "unreal" shadows that borrow their structure, efficacy, and value, from truly existing, immaterial Ideas. But this line of proof, though of great importance in the history of philosophy, need not be examined here. It becomes highly abstract and leads to no conclusive results, in the sense, that is, of agreement among those who occupy themselves with the problem.

To the argument that the universe shows the sort of design that only a conscious mind could order, it is answered that the order is no more than the mutual reactivity of the elements that compose the universe. Astrophysics has theories to account for the splendid stars and the satisfying arrangement of the solar system, and biology attempts to explain the evolution and interrelationship of living things. There are even suggestive theories, based on our new knowledge of genes, viruses, and large protein molecules, meant to bridge the gap between the nonliving and the living.

The most general refutation for the arguments for God's existence is not that they can be proved false, but that they involve unnecessary assumptions. Most of us are willing to grant that if a simple theory explains the facts, there is no need to accept a complicated one. In this case, the atheists say, not only is the theory more complicated, but it creates insuperable difficulties in grasping the presumed goodness of the presumed God. The theory of a God, they say, has no special advantage over the alternative, and is distinguished chiefly by the barren paradoxes it breeds and the cantankerous orthodoxies that adopt equally implausible and mutually exclusive versions of it.

But even this comprehensive refutation is not final. The believer denies that naturalism explains the facts as well as his philosophy does. He points out that every world view rests on unproved assumptions. Our relationship with the universe in which we are set appears to make it doubtful whether we can ever arrive at knowledge (other, some would claim, than mathematics) that escapes the taint of relativism. What is the color of the universe when seen through nonhuman organs sensitive to light? What would be the experience of a mind unlike the human except in its ability to receive and interpret stimuli in the light of consciousness? How can we jump out of ourselves to judge ourselves objectively? Surely the naturalistic description of "reality" is not beyond question. And if religious emotions and mystical insights never convince the unbeliever who finds it impossible to share them, they are often felt to be immune against the corrosive attacks of reason alone. Can one controvert the statement, "I am conscious of God" any more easily than the statement, "I am conscious of pain"? The mystic regards the rest of us as no more capable of refuting the presence of God than a blind man of refuting the presence of the colors he is constitutionally unable to sense. The mystic believer does not want to exchange his direct perception, as he conceives it to be, for a dubious metaphysics.

The psychic explanations we have been giving may seem aimed at establishing the practical usefulness of religion and its theoretical falsity. We have held, for example, that God and the Devil have a psychic source in the projection of our own impulses. But it is a mistake to suppose that the irrational impulsion of a belief proves it to be wrong. A person may have a deadly fear of traveling in airplanes, technically a phobia. All the reasons he gives for refusing to travel by plane are only rationalizations. Yet planes do crash, and no statistics on passenger miles flown safely can assure anyone that he will not be caught in an accident. While the deadly fear is irrationally motivated, in substance it may be as rational, as accurate in predicting the future, as the assurance based on statistics that apply to travelers in general but to no single traveler or occasion in particular. Who really knows who the next victim will be?

Neither the psychological character or origin of a belief proves it true or false. We may have come to believe that two times two equals four, because mothers give smiles and candy when we first recite the multiplication table, or because our minds have a tendency to certain rhythmic groupings. And yet two times two may really equal four. It can be demonstrated by generally acceptable methods that they do. Once our experience has led us to believe in a God, rational arguments (which may also act as rationalizations) cannot be offhandedly dismissed without direct rational refutation.

With respect to many religious claims, proof or disproof is something that psychiatry as such cannot undertake. It is a basic mistake, however, to suppose that psychiatry, or the other sciences, are altogether irrelevant to the truth of religion. It is easy enough to announce that we should render unto science that which belongs to it, and to religion whatever lies within its own proper sphere; but just as Caesar and God overlap, so do science and religion. Astronomy no longer allows us to believe that the world was created five or ten thousand years ago, even if an ingenious fellow can show that it might have been (God might conceivably have created a world that has every appearance of being older than it is). Paleontological data make it overwhelmingly hard to believe that man's body was literally shaped from the dust and not evolved from a succession of animals. Meteorology, agronomy, and medicine, show that it is highly improbable that each rainfall, good or bad crop, or disease, is the result of the special interposition of God's will into the causal enchainment of things. A wisely formulated religion must continue to adapt itself to verified knowledge. The heart of the fortress may remain the same, but because the outworks are always being destroyed they must also be rebuilt.

What direct effects does psychiatry have on the claim of religion to embody the truth? Freud expressed himself in a book whose title, *The Future of an Illusion,* gives away his attitude. Freud's theory, which we have repeated after him, is that the child creates gods, whom he fears and tries to propitiate but nevertheless entrusts with his welfare. The gods have three functions: to exorcise the terrors of nature, to reconcile man to the cruelty of fate, and to make amends for the painful restraints that communal life imposes.

These functions, says Freud, reveal themselves in historically developed dogma. The dogma demands to be believed on the grounds that our remote ancestors believed in it, and that we have proofs from antiquity. We are also forbidden to raise the question of truth at all. Society, to make such an interdiction, must understand how precarious are its religious claims. Rationally established truths need no defense against questioning.

According to Freud, then, religion is an illusion born of the believers' needs to see reality as colored by their wishes. Nor is the "God" of the "idealists" satisfactory, for He is

147

only a thin shadow of the mighty religious personage. While religion has checked the asocial instincts, it has had grave faults. The number of men who smart under the yoke of civilization is appallingly large; and we may doubt whether men were happier when religious doctrines ruled over all minds. It is sure that men were not more moral, for they have always known how to subvert religious precepts by conforming to them externally. And the priests have helped their flocks to escape by insisting that God is kind as well as just. Make an oblation, they told the sinner, and you are free to sin again. Religion has supported immorality too.

Therefore religion, says Freud, is the universal obsessional neurosis of humanity. It dominates man's thoughts and commands his actions irrationally. Instead of venturing into the hostile world he retires into childishness. We should rid ourselves of our illusion, admit honestly that everything in our culture is of purely human origin, and turn our energies toward the improvement of our lot. Science is the tool to use. It may be subjective in that it cannot be detached from human perceptions and thoughts. But it yields the information that is relevant to human needs. What science cannot give us we can get from no other source.

Freud is obviously a philosophic naturalist. His picture of the psychic roots of religion, which is substantially the one we have adopted, compels no one to declare that all the claims of religion are false. Neither the psychological character or origin of a belief proves it true or false. As for his argument from history, it is subject to the same intricate difficulties as other historical arguments that include the whole of human history in their sweep. There are too many controversial details. It is hardly possible to reconstruct history in the absence of religion, or with a drastically different religion, to ascertain how much better or worse or happier or unhappier men would have been. History does not lend itself to controlled experiments with communities identical except for their religions, experiments that might help us to decide exactly what effects religion has. Nor does the insufficiency of one kind of religion prove that all other kinds are insufficient. It is as if one were to say that historically governments have been bad, that is, that the governed have been unhappy and incompletely ethical; and therefore all government is bad. Or it is as if one were to say that everybody has indigestion at some time and many have it most of the time, and therefore food is proved to be bad. Compelling arguments have to be sharper than that.

Freud was not always as implacably rationalistic as he appears in *The Future of an Illusion*. His student, Theodor Reik, reports that Freud told him that whenever he had to reach a relatively unimportant decision, he weighed the evidence pro and con and accepted the rational conclusion that followed. But when it came to critical decisions, such as the choice of a wife or profession, he trusted to his deepest unconscious impulses.[1] In other words, Freud was willing to concede that where reasoning could not provide a satisfactory solution to a problem, our unconsciously motivated wishes might indeed do so.

Freud's famous pupil, Carl Jung, has shown the same independence of his teacher in judging religion as in the formulation of psychoanalytic principles. He leans far toward mysticism, and not a little, his detractors charge, towards mystification. Of the psychic usefulness of religion,

[1] Reik reports the conversation on page vii of his book, *Listening with the Third Ear*, New York, 1948.

Jung is sure. In his experience the proportion of devout neurotics has been extremely small. The symbolism of religion and the fantasies of patients are similar, and religious morality is an attempt like the ones that patients make to deal with the forces of their inner life, though it succeeds where they more often fail.

The present age has the urge, no doubt prompted by unconscious forces, to estimate the world in a matter-of-fact, empirical way, which is as arbitrary, symbolic, and metaphysical, as the older religious way. This, at any rate, is what Jung maintains, and he adds that since we have no idea of the manner in which the psychic may arise from the physical, it is just as well to assume that the psyche arises from a spiritual principle our understanding cannot penetrate. There is, we know, an inner self we are able to experience but never to define conceptually. It is a simultaneously known and unknown midpoint of psychic life toward which all our ultimate aims converge.

Our psychic life, according to Jung, is in a large measure collective. Metaphorically, the unconscious "is a collective human being combining the characteristics of both sexes, transcending youth and age, birth and death, and, from having at his command a human experience of one or two million years, almost immortal."[2] That is, the brain structure, or the psychic structure, of human beings has common properties acquired through a heredity that conserves an immense past. The collective unconscious is less like a person than an endlessly moving stream that carries figures and images into our consciousness during dreams and abnormal states of mind. The uniformity of the collective unconscious is demonstrated by the approximate uniformity of figures, signs, and images, which reappear in all

[2] Carl Jung, *Modern Man in Search of a Soul*, New York, 1947 (reprint of English edition of 1933), p. 215.

times and cultures as well as in the fantasies of individuals. Consciousness and rationality are relatively new and weak, and the unconscious seizes power easily. Whenever the psychic danger is great, instinctive defense mechanisms come into play and signalize their activities by the helpful images that ascend into consciousness. The unconscious has an instinctive wisdom of its own, and unless we come to terms with it and draw on the reserves of its wisdom and strength, we can never be whole, happy, or truly productive.

Jung does not hesitate to say that although an individual consciousness may be cut off from ourselves by death, it is doubtful whether the continuity of the psychic processes is broken by death, for we are not at all assured that the psyche is chained to the brain. He does not hesitate to speak of the "will of God," nor to write that the living spirit "freely chooses the men in whom it lives and who proclaim it. This living spirit is eternally renewed and pursues its goal in manifold and inconceivable ways throughout the history of mankind. Measured against it, the names and forms which men have given it mean little enough; they are only the changing leaves and blossoms on the stem of the eternal tree."[3]

Jung is thus no skeptic who derides faith in higher powers. If we restrict the meaning of God to our unconscious psychic reserves and the endless energy, transcending individuals, that manifests itself within and without the psyche, or if we mean by God our intuitive insights and higher selves, then Jung agrees that there is a God. But the existence of God in a final, metaphysical, transcendental sense is quite beyond the power of the human mind to prove or disprove. Yet we believe in a transcendental God. Our psyche demands that the internal and external chaos

[3] *Op. cit.*, p. 282.

be resolved into intelligibility. What consciousness cannot decide, the unconscious has decided for us, since the unconscious contains the primeval, archetypal idea-image of an omnipotent existence. If we consciously repudiate God, we usually replace Him by a less adequate psychic substitute that continues to fill the same psychic role.

What do these ideas of Jung add up to? Arguments about the metaphysical God are futile. But the psyche may well live on indefinitely. The submerged bulk of the psyche is collective and supraindividual. Its experiences have caused it to form the image of God, in whom we must believe even when we appear to deny Him. There is no one form of belief that fits men in general. Some are better off as Catholics, some as Protestants, some as Hindus. But to be a conscious unbeliever—a state of mind also motivated by irrational forces—is to invite psychic disaster. In fine, Jung urges us to accept the belief we cannot really root out of ourselves. If the intellect cannot quite believe, the will is able to almost by itself.

If we omit consideration of the metaphysical issues, the controversy between Freud and Jung reduces itself to this: Freud believes that religion is a seductive method, akin to neurosis, for shirking the issues and efforts of life, while Jung believes that religion is inevitable and indispensable, and that irreligion is akin to neurosis because it is an attempt to deny the unity of the self, the continuity of the conscious with the unconscious, and of the psyche with the universe. To Freud, the religious person manifests the continued illusions of the child, to Jung, the cumulated wisdom of mankind.

In our opinion, everything depends not on the bare issue of religion or irreligion, but on the quality of the religion or irreligion. Both the atheist and the believer may be stupid, insensitive, superstitious, and antisocial; and both may be intelligent, sensitive, enlightened, and socially helpful. While it is true that inflexible dogma, at irrevocable odds with science, may induce peace of mind, it does so at a heavy price, the price of an undermined intelligence and an at least latent antagonism to anyone who does not share the dogma. If the course of history has made anything clear, it is that society, the little and the great alike, has a desperate need for intelligent compromise. But if we refuse to entertain hypotheses that seem repugnant to begin with, we can never gain the freedom and flexibility that distinguish reason from instinct, nor achieve that organic suspicion of our own opinions that is the most effective agent of intelligent compromise.

On the basis of such reasoning, and without reference, necessarily, to ultimate truth, a distinction may be drawn between good and bad religion. Religion, as we hope we have made clear, tends to keep us optimistic and ethical, and it is this function that explains the survival of religion from a social point of view. But it does not take a long excursion into history to discover that religion can incite despair, suicide, cruelty, idiotic intransigence, and warfare. In the eyes of someone, each of us is an infidel whose soul must be subjugated; and we are lucky if he does not think in his innermost mind that to capture our souls he must batter down the obstructive walls of our bodies. The God-Father-Superego harbors elements of sadism, masochism, and other aggressiveness.

Still, it is a mistake to judge religions simple-mindedly by their outward appearance, without an understanding of the particular nuances of their nature and the circumstances of their development. That a religion has lasted a thousand years or more and governed great numbers of men is *prima facie* evidence that it has been of psychic use. Hinduism is often attacked as having denied the value of life. From the point of view of most of us, it has. The same should be said of many of the ascetics and mystics of the other religions, and of those who held with a tenacious and dour pleasure to their conviction that men have, since Adam, been born to be damned. But if the whole rather chaotic structure of Hinduism is examined, a more temperate evaluation must be made. The multiplied hands of the gods, the sanctity of the cow, the exuberant surfaces of the temples, the ceremonies of thanksgiving, the craftsman's worship of his tools and the farmer's of his implements, are tributes to life and not death. If it is death the Hindu worships, it is an extraordinarily fecund death, concerned with the minute regulation of its lively children. Utter self-abnegation in a wandering celibacy is supposed to be the climax of a disciplined life as a student, householder, and meditative dweller in the forest. Under the conditions that have prevailed in India—and elsewhere—a substantial measure of resignation and a feeling of the unreality of material things have been useful, intelligent adaptations to a difficult state of affairs.

Although, therefore, we distinguish between good and bad religions on the grounds of their social usefulness, ignorant condemnation cannot be taken seriously. Perhaps the wisest approach to religion is through an attitude that is characteristic of the most enlightened Hinduism. The manifold gods, devils, duties, and ceremonials, and the religions in which they are embodied, are different symbolical expressions for the same basic experience. As we are now aware, even the theories of the physical sciences are somewhat arbitrary, and are constantly being replaced by theories refined in the light of more extensive facts, or modified for the sake of greater consistency or scope. What is common to such sciences is not this or that particular theory, but the systematic caution with which the evidence is gathered and the rigor with which the evidence is subsumed under general principles. What is common to religion is not a particular dogma, but the systematic use of psychosocial mechanisms to dissipate and exploit guilt, restrain destructive impulses, and foster an ethical sense. The metaphysical beliefs we hold vary from century to century. Now we believe that a malignant spirit lives in the boulder that falls and endangers us, now that God requires the blood of an animal to appease His wrath, now that the angels form a literal if immaterial choir of praise to their Lord, now that God is the manifest energy of the universal process. Or we may believe that He is the highest of the hierarchy of values emerging out of the universal matrix, or the actualizer of possibilities, or the eternal penumbra of mystery in which man is fated to grope. The particular metaphors in which we define our experience always change, but there never is any change in the need of society to enlist the conscience of its members, or of the individual to believe more than he can prove.

Believing is almost as necessary to humans as eating. What is believed is of course not necessarily useful, any more than what is eaten is always nourishing. But belief is essential to the efficient functioning of a human organism, and this belief is more than the elementary faith, implicit in all the actions of a sane man, that effect follows cause, that there are other persons besides himself, and that he can distinguish between his dreaming and his waking life. We have the need to believe, and it is futile to think that many of us can be happy though thoroughly skeptical. One of the most usual, personally useful, and mistaken beliefs that philosophers or scientists may hold is that they arrive at their philosophical conclusions on strictly rational grounds. The belief is personally useful but socially dangerous.

There is nothing in this book or in psychiatry that is a sufficient argument for or against the acceptance of any faith, if the faith is not contrary to whatever has been rigorously verified. We do not wish to recommend or disparage religion, except to the extent that effective social motivation has religious aspects.

We have confined ourselves to the general nature and content of religious belief and never tried to advise the individual what his attitudes toward religion should be. The individual's acceptance or rejection of faith or duty does not depend on his knowledge of a good argument pro or con. The religious attitudes of most people are determined by other than purely religious considerations. Especially because religion helps to maintain society, there is social pressure for a conforming religious affiliation. Yet in certain ways society may tolerate great latitude within the sphere of religious observance. It is just here that the individual finds a convenient stage on which to act out his unconscious, or occasionally conscious wish to rebel against society. It is also a stage for the expression of one's filial attitudes, since the acceptance of religious authority is psychically derived from that of parental authority. It is therefore a stage for the working out of the deeply embedded, conflicting wishes for submission to parental authority and rejection of it, wishes that utilize not only the content of religion, but also the parents' own religious feelings. Against such unconscious forces, whether beneficent or not, rational arguments are of little avail. However, rationality still has its place and its work to do. Although it is hard to accept Freud's belief that faith can be utterly superseded, faith can be guided by reason.

It is reason that tells us that agnosticism or strict rationality is possible on some points, but not on most of those that establish the structure of living. Even if a conviction is approximately rational, the intensity with which it is held may not be. John Dewey opposes the traditional religions, but he wants to transfer their faith to faith in the good results of reason applied pragmatically to human problems. But reason alone cannot prove to an individual that it is best for him under every circumstance to surrender to the social good. If you can evade paying part of the income tax and run almost no risk of being caught, is there any persuasive reason not to? Put the cash into your pocket. No one will be the wiser, and you, your wife, and your children, will be the happier. And if you can get a safe job at a desk instead of going to the front lines, is there any persuasive reason not to? After all, you owe it to your wife and children to watch attentively over your well-being. If everyone acted selfishly, matters would go worse than they do, but the selfish person, who knows that there are others like him, is realistically aware that there are many timid or unselfish persons of whom he can take advantage. Reason, reduced to its elementary protective function, may very well counsel selfishness, and reason may be unable to agree with optimistic predictions of the future. Dewey is therefore inviting an unrationally conscientious devotion to reason in the service of mankind. If his faith is to be propagated effectively, it needs to draw on or develop a tradition, to instill itself into the agencies that shape the superego, and to develop appropriate rituals. If it were to be supported by these, it would be a religion.

Granting that psychoanalysis can rid us of unconscious guilt and so usurp the old office of religion, what is there in psychoanalysis to inspire optimism and morality? The compulsive symptoms of neurosis may vanish in the face of understanding, as Freud hopes that religious ritual will vanish. But society needs compulsions. Since there is no rational estimate of the future sufficient to justify optimism, this emotion on which society depends must be evoked irrationally. Our preferences, our very desire to live, are irrational, and their character is not the calculated result of any mental arithmetic. Reason by itself could not have inspired Freud's reverence for the truth, or his own unrelaxing and remarkably high personal ethical standards. It could not have produced the line of the broken bodies of his fellow Jews that marched into the gas chambers chanting, "I believe with a whole faith in the coming of the Messiah, and though he linger, yet I will await his coming every day."

Freud states that analysis often strikes a factor so resistant that it undoes the attempt at therapy. It strikes an unconscious need for punishment related to masochism, and derived, according to Freud, from the death instinct, which has become directed against itself. But the impulse that psychoanalysis is unable to overcome may be diverted by a good religion to socially useful purposes. Good causes, too, have martyrs. The case of humans would be much closer to hopeless if there were no social reformers to invite the trouble that meeker and no less rational men shy away from.

For society to remain alive, it must feed on emotion. For an individual to remain happy, and even alive, maybe, he must hold some unrational or unrationally intense belief. If we are to use the pragmatic criterion according to which a belief is true if it helps the organism to maintain itself efficiently, then many at least superficially incompatible beliefs can be true, though perhaps unequally true, or one can be true at one time or for one person, and another at another time or for another person. It might be less confusing to say that the impulse to believe is such that it must accept the truth of some of its objects, which are therefore true so far as the person at the moment is concerned.

The pragmatic criterion of truth need not be accepted, or may be interpreted otherwise, but that does not change the basic point, which is that we are subject to a nearly irresistible need to believe. The need we can escape only in so far as we can avoid infancy and childhood, a detour too extravagant for most of us to make, and in so far as we can discover utterly objective guiding truths and values, a discovery the merely human among us find too difficult to accomplish. The dissipation of guilt is not an intellectual process. Ambition, devotion, love, and hatred, are not intellectual. Of the many illusions to which reason is subject, one of the most persistent and endangering is the illusion that it is the master. Reason is only the luminous tip of a massive and impulsive subterranean psyche. If it is to make the best of the powers it has and cast its light back into the dim psyche out of which it has emerged, it must make of itself a humiliated light. It may humiliate reason to acknowledge that it must serve irrational desires, discipline itself in the permissive prohibitions of ritual, and sustain itself with faith. But to refuse to acknowledge its needs would be still more humiliating, because it would be an avowal that reason could not even see, much less govern, its nature. And the last word of reason is that the shame is born of a false pride, the pride that goeth before a fall. "When pride cometh, then cometh shame. But with the lowly is wisdom."

Index

161